EROS PEREIRA

**CIVIL RESPONSIBILITY FOR
DENTISTRY MALPRACTICE**

2 Ed. – English - 2022

EROS PEREIRA

CIVIL RESPONSIBILITY FOR DENTISTRY MALPRACTICE

<u>Concentration Area</u>: Principles and Guarantees Constitutional Laws and their Reflections on Legislation Citizenship Protection Agency.

EROS PEREIRA

To my advisor, Dr. José Luiz Gavião de Almeida.

To my teachers and students.

To my master's colleagues

To the director of the Special Court Cível de Campinas- Annex UNIP.

To the Librarian Rosana of the Paulista University - UNIP- Campus Vitale-Campinas.

To Gil, coordinator of the Pedagogy Library of Unicamp.

To employee Jose of the Faculty of Pedagogy of Unicamp for the valuable books.

To my family.

To Vania, Luke, Mirella, and Matthew for so many joys.

THANKS

My special thanks to the

Professor Dr. José Luiz Gavião de Almeida

for teachings, guidance and

by the example of dedication.

It is a great example for professionals

of law, in addition to a great master and

friend.

"The real villains are anger, envy, impatience, and intolerance. With them, problems cannot be solved. Although we may have temporary success, ultimately intolerance or anger will create for us, more difficulties. Anger is for instant solutions. However, when we try to solve problems with compassion, sincerity, and availability, our solutions may take longer to find, but ultimately they will be of the best quality."

Dalai Lama

SUMMARY

The present work aims to study the civil liability of the dental surgeon concerning the Constitutional provisions and Consumer Protection Code, Civil Code, and other legislation, in the case of dental error, verifying the professional's responsibility through his guilt. A dental mistake occurs when the oral health professional acts with recklessness, malpractice, or negligence by himself or the front of someone under his responsibility and because of his work. There is a whole technique to be followed by the professional, from sterilization to the constant study of innovations in the area of activity, always using the method that brings better results. The Federal Constitution of 1988 holds health professionals accountable, including the dental surgeon. Because of this responsibility, the professional must be attentive to all the necessary documentation. It is essential to have proof that the treatment performed was done according to the correct standards of the specialty. In addition, considering the poor intervention of the professional, the Consumer Protection Code, Law 8078 of September 11, 1990, establishes the dentist's responsibility for dental malpractice. After analyzing the laws that regulate the profession, the present work seeks to study the various cases of dental errors in the multiple specialties that the domain allows. The work used the empirical research in the Special Civil Court of Campinas - Annex UNIP - to survey how the search for compensation resulting from dental errors and, also, the theoretical analysis in books related to the subject and survey

documental, analyzing sentences of the magistrates, to see how is the current understanding about the various law process in dental specialties. Another aspect researched refers to

the determination of guilt and the multiple factors that must be raised to determine professional responsibility in case of patient cooperation or choices for more accessible treatments. However, they are not the most indicated. It is expected that this work can be a valuable source of consultation with legal professionals, dental professionals, and other stakeholders.

ABSTRACT

The objective of the present work is to study the civil responsibility of the dentist surgeon front to the Constitutional devices and Consumer Defense Code, Civil Code, and other legislation, in the case of the dentist's malpractice, verifying the professional responsibilities through his blame. The dentist's malpractice happens when the professional of the buccal health area, the dentist surgeon acts with imprudence, mistake or negligence for himself or somebody's action under his responsibility in his work place. The whole technique exists to be followed by the professional, from sterilization to the constant study of the innovations in the area of performance, always using the method that brings better results. The Federal Constitution of 1988 makes health area professionals responsible, including dentist surgeons, and establishes its demand. Facing this responsibility, the professional should be attentive to every act and every necessary documentation to prove that the accomplished treatment was made in agreement with the correct norms of the specialty. Besides, considering the professional's wrong intervention, the Consumer Defense Code, Law 8078, establishes the dentist's responsibility for the malpractice. After analyzing the laws that regulate the profession, the present work tries to study several cases of dentist malpractice in several specialties.

TABLE OF CONTENTS

INTRODUCTION
1 LEGISLATIVE HISTORY
   1.1 Foreign legislation
   1.2 Brazilian legislation
      1.2.1 In the Federal Constitution of 1988
      1.2.2 No Civil Code
      1.2.3 In the Code of Dental Ethics
      1.2.4 In the Consumer Protection Code
      1.2.5 Federal and state health laws
      1.2.6 No Criminal Code
   1.3 The dental professional

2 CIVIL LIABILITY
    1. Concept
    2. Subjective and objective responsibility
    3. Contractual and extracontractual liability
    4. The obligation of medium and resultado
    5. The dentist's civil liability

3 SPECIES OF GUILT
3.1 Civil liability with culpa
    3.1.1 Negligence
    3.1.2 Recklessness
    3.1.3 Malpractice
  3.2 Deceit acts
  3.3 Civil guilt, criminal and administrative guilt
    3.3.1 Omission of first aid
    3.3.2 Corporalesions
    3.3.3 Accident Murder
    3.3.4 Intentional murder
 3.4 The causal relationship between the condition and the harmful result
 3.5 Prova burden
 3.6 Exclusions of responsability
 3.7 The informed consent

4 AESTHETIC AND FUNCTIONAL DAMAGE
    1. Orthodontics and ATM
    2. Implantodontia
    3. Dentária prosthesis
    4. Endodontics
    5. Aesthetic and restorative dentistry

6. Maxillomaxilla-facial surgery
7. Periodontics
8. Radiology
9. **Buccal** pathology/**semiology**
10. Odontopediatrics

11. Dental anesthesia
12. Social Dentistry
13. Stomatology

5 THE INSURANCE FOR MORAL AND MATERIAL DAMAGE
6 FEITA RESEARCH IN THE SPECIAL CIVIL COURT FINAL CONSIDERATIONS
REFERENCES
VOCABULARY
ANNEX TO LEGISLATION
A - Federal Constitution
B - Law 5,081 of August 24, 1966
C - Resolution No. 185 of April 26, 1993
D - Health Code of São Paulo (art.22 to 32
E - Consolidation of standards for proceedings in regional councils (Dec. Issue 68,704 of June 3, 1971
F - Code of Dental Ethics
G - Jurisprudence
H - Cases of dental errors in the foreigner
  – *Nerve damage from bone Graf surgery*
  - *Dentists keep a cautious eye on IOM recommendations*
  – *The Redwoods Group Dentists Insurance Program*
About the Author

INTRODUCTION

Modern life and the relationship of consumption that encompasses the health network has charged greater responsibility to all, including dental acts and errors.

The present work aims to demonstrate what doctrine and jurisprudence say on the subject. At first, it is observed that there is a scarcity of studies on dental responsibility. Perhaps this is because of the most significant repercussion of errors and the consequent medical commitment.

The subject is of great relevance given the increased demand for dental treatments. Either by reducing their costs, by the increase in the number of agreements that proliferate today in companies, or even because of the importance that people have given to oral health. Either for a better aesthetic appearance or simply by the search for the preservation of dental elements.

It is relevant to the increase in life expectancy in Brazil, finding older people still with all their teeth, valuing them as if they were pearls for well-being in their lives.

Thus, people began to care more about tooth loss or health impairment resulting from dental treatment, seeking compensation and accountability of the profession in case of damage.

At the time of the bibliographic survey, we verified the existence of a relatively small number of national works. In Brazil, the reinput of medical error was written, as mentioned.

Lutz[1] wrote the first monograph on the subject in Brazil to warn dental professionals about the dangers of the activity they perform. He reports that all countries had civil and criminal legislation applicable to negligence, malpractice, and recklessness at the time of the monograph.

Due to the scarcity of work on the damage caused in dental activity, we will also use jobs related to medical error, considering that there are better-defined means and result obligations, similar to what occurs in dentistry and the fact of Art. 951 of the Civil Code (CC) reports that the professional should indemnify cases of negligence, recklessness, and malpractice resulting from their professional activity, not differentiating between the branches of professional health activity.

Arbenz[2] dealt with the doctor's responsibility, and by extension, that of the dentist, adapting medical absences to dentistry. As we will show below, the responsibility for the acts of the dentist is founded on guilt, as is usually medical responsibility.

The relationship between the dentist and his patient results from a contract, which may be verbal or written, generating administrative, civil, criminal, and ethical liability, as the case may be. It will be shown that the professional's responsibility for the acts performed in the exercise of dentistry is usually of the medium and maybe of the result.

Currently, society is increasingly aware of its rights and attentive to the actions of professionals who are subject to answer lawsuits, even if they are exercising their professions diligently and with zeal.

---

[1] LUTZ, Gualter. The. Errors and Accidents in Dentistry. Rio de Janeiro, 1938 *Apud* FRANÇA, Beatriz Helena Sottile. **Civil and Criminal Liability of the Dentist**. 1993. Thesis (Master's degree in Legal Dentistry and Deontology) - School of Dentistry, State University of Campinas, Piracicaba.

[2] ARBENZ, William Oswaldo. Professional responsibility of the dentist. *In*: FRANCE, Beatriz Helena Sottile. **Civil and Criminal Liability of the Dentist**. 1993. Thesis (Master's degree in Legal Dentistry and Deontology) - School of Dentistry, State University of Campinas, Piracicaba.

The dentist has a very similar function to the lawyer because he carries out his activity personally, with autonomy to practice his knowledge. Its position is directly linked to its name.

Dentists need to be better equipped with the necessary precautions, legally, documentary, and professionally, with recycling of learning and constant updating, because the professional can be held responsible even for not using the most advanced technique if it was available at the time of the work.

With the main objective of analyzing the civil liability of the dentist, we will explore several peculiar aspects of the profession later.

We will seek to discuss the relationship between the dentist, acting as a service provider, and the patient, a consumer following the Consumer Protection Code, and its legal implications in the case of unsuccessful treatments.

Has the professional's relationship with his patient, inspired mainly by trust, become only a consumer relationship where the patient likes or dislikes the product and wants his money back if he doesn't like it? How will the dentist get the product delivered if it is a service provider?

Consumer rights extend to compensation for damage caused by the dentist's action or omission. Every professional should be aware of the laws that hold him accountable. His jurisdiction is still the factor that will leave him most away from the courts. But in addition to your scientific and technical knowledge, you need to be aware of the rights and duties of patients and each member working in your office or team.

We will try to clarify, among other doubts, whether or not the actions against dentists have increased, which specialties generate the most significant conflict and the average value of the causes.

We want to see to what extent the professional is responsible in his day-to-day for the successes of their performance and how the reality of the Brazilian's financial situation influences the choice of professionals and treatments to understand why professionals should not respond equally to setbacks. Account should be taken of the various factors involved.

Conclusion: there are factors such as poor patient hygiene and patients who only seek the professionals when the dental element is already significantly compromised. They hope that because it pays the price, they can have the right product; that is, by paying for the treatment, the dentist must restore his tooth to the actual situation of a healthy and perfect tooth.

We need to clarify whether it is possible to charge the dentist an objective result in the face of different realities. Realities such as that of the plastic surgeon, who can be condemned for not achieving a perfect surgical result, even in the case of an unexpected tissue scar; science has already shown that tissue regeneration varies significantly from individual to individual.

All these realities must be clarified through a statistical study and recent information from science to demonstrate the extent to which the professional should be held accountable, mainly because the Consumer Protection Code says that the responsibility of liberal professionals will be done by proving their guilt.

We will address the importance of the awareness of dental professionals and their civil liability, the quality of their services, and clarifications of the professionals of the legal world on the details of a biological system, how we are, and the social implications of the dentist's activity.

We want to demonstrate that obtaining appropriate treatments simply by punishing laws will not achieve the goal of better dentistry or better preparation of professionals for fear of lawsuits, but awareness both by dentists of the legal aspects of their profession, as well as in the legal world of the socio-economic characteristics of the career of the dentist and the realities of the patients who seek them.

Suppose we achieve awareness in the legal sphere, which cannot be considered all the acts of the dentist as being of the obligation of result, due to several factors that will be commented on, clarify the dental professionals of their civil responsibilities and an awareness that will be held responsible through their guilt. In that case, we will be pleased to have collaborated in some way for the prevention and solution of the issues.

The effectiveness of constitutional rules established through unconstitutional legislation will be addressed, ensuring the execution of what is in the more significant norm.

This work sought to see the constitutional reflexes in private law by analyzing the constitutional protection of health through history and the evolution of The Obligation Alright in the Civil Code, Consumer Protection Code, and constitutional commands in the face of civil liability for dental error.

We tried to contribute, although modest, to the study of Civil Liability for Dental Error and, who knows, to support future studies on the subject.

1 LEGISLATIVE HISTORY

In this chapter, we will seek to synthesize foreign legislation, which deals with civil liability, referring to dental treatments throughout history, including as the subject was treated in Brazil until reaching the laws in force in the national order and its applications.

1.1 Foreign legislation

The art of healing has always been sought after since the most remote times. It was linked to religious beliefs and systems. The ancient civilizations, in codifying their laws, already spoke of the responsibility of the therapist.[3]

---

[3] Lutz, Adolpho Gualter. **Mistakes and accidents in dentistry**. Ed. Mr. C.Mendes. Rio de Janeiro, p.09, 1938.

To better understand the civil liability arising from medical and, by similarity, dental, we will make a brief history for a greater understanding of the different aspects that involve civil liability, to know its origins until reaching the current legislations.

Medicine was essentially artisanal in its early days. Healing had an aspect of healing linked to divine gifts. The doctors were faithful priests, but in the event of failure, the punishment was severe.[4]

In the sixteenth century, the investigation of medical damage begins, with legal codifications requiring medical expertise in legal procedures, constituting the beginnings of legal medicine.[5]

In Hammurabi's reign more than 40 centuries ago, the life-saving surgeon should receive ten silver coins, but if the person died, he would have both hands severed. Dental infections were already cured with applications of medication and resin.[6]

Kfouri Neto says in his book:[7]

> The first historical document dealing with the problem of medical error is the Code of Hammurabi (1790-1770.C), which also contains exciting norms regarding the medical profession in general. Suffice it to say that some articles of this law (215 n.s.) established, for complex operations, compensation for the work, which was up to the doctor. In parallel, in subsequent articles, the surgeon was required to pay the utmost attention and expertise in the practice of the profession; otherwise, severe penalties were triggered that went to the amputation of the hand of the expert (or unfortunate) doctor. Such sanctions were applied when death or injury occurred to the patient due to malpractice or malpractice, and compensation for the damage was foreseen when an enslaved person or animal was poorly cured. Thus, it is evident that the concept of guilt did not exist, in a modern legal sense, while objective responsibility was in force coincident with the current notion: if the patient died after the surgical intervention, the doctor killed him – and should be punished. In a sense, at that time, the surgeon could not say, with particular professional satisfaction, as he does today: the operation was very successful, but the patient is dead. If this was the law, Avecone continues - one can imagine with what serenity the doctor was preparing for surgery, with the means of which he then had. But, of course,

---

[4] DANTAS, Eduardo Vasconcelos dos Santos. **Historical Aspects of Medical Civil Liability.** Available in:<http://www.jusvi.com. >. Accessed 11/08/2003, p. 01.

[5] DÓRIA, Rodrigues. Medical Responsibility apud LUTZ, Gualter Adolpho. **Mistakes and accidents in dentistry**. Ed. Mr. C.Mendes. Rio de Janeiro, p.10,1938.
[6] *Ibid.*, p. 09.
[7] KFOURI NETO, Miguel. **Medical Liability,** 4th ed., p. 38. Sao Paulo. Ed. RT, 2000.

only extreme simplicity operations were practiced because anatomy was very little known.

The Law of Moses in chapter XXI of Exodus, see. 18 et to follow, talks about reparation for bodily harm known as the Law of Talion. In this period, there were also the Bognazkeni Tablets, dated 1290 bc.[8]

At this time, Michna arose, of Jewish origin, citing several laws that are not private or originating from this person in the form of code. His tenth law deals with *the Nezikin,* or *Rhalabah* (in Hebrew), which means damage.

In Egypt, the priests were doctors and were given the name sunu. The Greek historian Diodorus of Sicily found that the Egyptians had a book containing the precepts of medical art, where the consequences for error could be the most serious.[9]

Little is known about the golden age of Greece and the condemnation of the crucifix of the doctor of Efestion, whose name was Glauco, condemned by King Alexander the Great. Later some elements overlap with the vengeful concept of Talião's Law.[10]

Studies have been developed that have given medicine a more scientific character. These studies would become the *Corpus Hippocraticum*. Advances in the medical system allowed changes in the calculation of responsibilities. Now the medical professional has come to be held accountable for the result itself, but his professional conduct in the specific case.[11]

Medical guilt would be cleared through a collegiate. It would only be declared if there was inattention to the precepts or non-compliance with the medical-sanitary practices and procedures.

A General Reparation Law was created in Athens, which treated men unequally, distinguishing the involuntary (culpable) damage. A determined indemnity corresponded,

---

[8]DANTAS, Eduardo Vasconcelos dos Santos. **Historical Aspects of Medical Civil Liability.** São Paulo, 2002. Available in**:** < http://www.jusvi.com>. Accessed 11/08/2003, p. 04.
[9]Lutz, Adolpho Gualter. **Mistakes and accidents in dentistry**. Ed. Mr. C.Mendes. Rio de Janeiro, p.09,1938.
[10]*Ibid.*, p. 10.
[11]DANTAS, Eduardo Vasconcelos dos Santos. **Historical Aspects of Medical Civil Liability**. São Paulo, 2002.Available in:< http://www.jusvi.com>. Accessed 11/08/2003, p. 08.

from voluntary (deceitful) damage, with compensation equivalent to twice that due for unintentional damage.

Plato participated in the innovation of the Law of Talion. It was based on philosophical ideas that the compensatory amount to be paid could lead to the transformation of hatred into friendship by developing the concept of aesthetic damage through the following concepts: in case of attempted murder resulting only in injuries, the offender would be ordered to repay the victim in an amount "X"; if the injury attempt was successful, it should pay double. You'd pay triple if you wanted to produce damage and leave an aesthetic sequel. If the cosmetic injury were incurable, the indemnity payment would be quadruple.[12]

The first Invalid Assistance Organization arose in Greece.

The principles of responsibility for the harm caused have emerged in Rome without the will to harm, without deceit, but only with guilt, which stems from negligence, malpractice, or recklessness. Lex Aquilia was promulgated at this time, dealing with numerous hypotheses of damage resulting from lack of care.[13]

Kfouri talks about how the subject was handled in Rome: [14]

> The Cornelia Law included several offenses related to the practice of the medical profession and the penalties that should be comminated. However, with *the lex Aquilia de damno*, a referendum after the Hydrangea Law of the third-century a.C., a concept of guilt was formulated, as well as some kinds of crimes that doctors could commit, such as the abandonment of the patient, the refusal to provide care, the errors derived from malpractice and dangerous experiences. As a consequence, the obligation to repair the damage is established, limiting it to economic damage, without considering what is now defined as moral damage. Whoever killed a slave or animal of others would be ordered to pay the highest amount he had in the year before the offense; whoever had injured an enslaved person or an animal of others, as well as destroyed or deteriorated other people's bodies, should pay the owner the highest amount that the object had in the 30 days preceding the offense. To bring *the action legis Aquiline*, it was necessary: a) that the damage had caused injury, that is, contrary to the right; b) a positive lack (*in committendo*). Letting the slave of others starve to death because it constituted *guilt in omission* did not generate responsibility. Any fault attributable to the author was sufficient: *in lege Aquilia, et levíssimo culpa venit*; c) a damage *corpori corpore datum* – the damage should have been caused by contact directly from the body of the author with that of the

---

[12] DANTAS, Eduardo Vasconcelos dos Santos. **Historical Aspects of Medical Civil Liability**. São Paulo, 2002. Available in:< http://www.jusvi.com>. Accessed 11/08/2003, p. 09.
[13] *Ibid.*, p. 06.
[14] KFOURI NETO, Miguel. **Medical Liability**, 4th ed.. Sao Paulo. Ed. RT, p.39, 2000.

> victim. "At *Lex Aquilia* is the first rudiments of medical responsibility, providing for the death penalty or deportation of the doctor guilty of professional misconduct. In Pliny's works, however, there are complaints of medical impunity because of the difficulty of the legal typifications already at that time. Ulpiano stated (Dig. 1, 18, 6, 7) that 'just as the physician should not be charged with the death, he must be charged with what has been committed by malpractice.' More than 1,500 years ago, the doctor was already under the commission, who became responsible for the damage he would cause to the patient due to lack of skill or knowledge.

For the Aquilian Law, there was no price for the free man, but the enslaved person had its value in coins. The indemnity should be at a fair price. The injured man was the value of the injury, and the judge decided whether the deal was appropriate or not. The destiny suit was worth twice as much as the manly.[15]

There was an important legislative development in the year 451 to .C., introducing the criminal penalty for personal injury cases, taking into account the individual qualification, the physical state of the injured, medical expenses, the notion of temporary disability, etc., influencing even the Napoleonic Code.[16]

The *Corpus Juries Civilis* was the laws collected from the Aquília Law by Justinian. The book Digesto contained the civil materials, indicating how to measure property and off-balance sheet losses.

This law spoke of damage to saleable things that possessed property rights, such as an enslaved person, and jurisprudence extended its application to every free man. According to Roman law, it was not up to the doctor to blame for the patient's natural death but for the results of his malpractice. The Romans also emerged the concept that great negligence matters in guilt and excessive negligence in great guilt, and may indeed matter.[17]

During the Middle Ages, canon law was formed, where the doctor's guilt for the death of someone is never presumed by the mere fact of dying a patient. Between 1173 and 1180, an anonymous jurist coded the law of the time in the "*Livre des assizes de la Cour des*

---

[15] KFOURI NETO, Miguel. **Medical Liability**, 4th ed.. Sao Paulo. Ed. RT, p.40, 2000.
[16] DANTAS, Eduardo Vasconcelos dos Santos. **Historical Aspects of Medical Civil Liability.** São Paulo, 2002. Available in: < http://www.jusvi.com >.. Accessed 11/08/2003, p. 07.
[17] Lutz, Adolpho Gualter. **Mistakes and accidents in dentistry.** Ed. Mr. C.Mendes. Rio de Janeiro, p.11, 1938.

Bourgeois," treating professionals who medicate or operate on injured in an undue manner, causing them to die.

The feathers were inhumane, like leading the doctor to whip through the city, wielding a urinal, and then be hanged. The fees received from the deceased were taken from the professional's estate and returned to the relatives of the dead patient. If mutilation resulted, the penalty would be for the disappointment of the right hand at the wrist level.[18] The Corte of Justice should still kick him out of town.

There are no specific provisions in the laws of the Latin Kingdom of Jerusalem on dental treatment, perhaps because, at the time, dental treatment was not separated from any other part of the body. Still, those who practiced them would be subject to the same legal provisions.

After the middle ages came to *the Constitutio Criminalis* Carolingeo, the Penal Code of Emperor Charles V in 1532, where he dealt with malpractice and negligence.[19]

Between the Middle Ages and the French revolution, there was a derogation from professional responsibility already in the modern age. The parliament francês declared the doctors and surgeons not responsible for the accidents that occur during treatment, but subsequent legal decisions maintained the professional, criminal and civil responsibilities.

In Anglo-Saxon countries, the law is divided into Usual Law and the Law of Written Laws. The Usual Law ("Common Law") decides the issues based on jurisprudence. According to him, extreme guilt can be compared to deceit. As each American state has a usual right, it follows that most malpractice lawsuits are judged in the civil forum and not in the criminal.

Almost all countries have civil legislation and criminal legislation applicable to recklessness, malpractice, and negligence, such as Germany, Argentina, Chile, Spain, France, Holanda, Honduras, Italy, Mexico, etc. These laws apply to both doctors and dentists.[20]

---

[18] Lutz, Adolpho Gualter. **Mistakes and accidents in dentistry**. Ed. Mr. C.Mendes. Rio de Janeiro, p.13,1938.
[19] *Ibid.*, p.14.
[20] Lutz, Adolpho Gualter. **Mistakes and accidents in dentistry**. Ed. Mr. C.Mendes. Rio de Janeiro, p.15, 1938.

In 1829, the French courts found it difficult to hold the doctor accountable. The burden of proof fell on those who accused the professional. In 1832 the first trial found a doctor guilty of mutilating a child during childbirth, having to pay an annual pension to the victim.[21]

Then came the concept of the loss of a chance: the medical error resulting from the fact that the patient was not offered all the options of cure. This loss would be enough to give professional responsibility. The first conviction based on this principle took place in France in 1957.

In 1947, the Nuremberg Code, a consequence of the war crimes that occurred, maintained the rights established in previous laws and set free consent with prior information on risk and benefit, showing for the first time the protection against biological material harm to the patient.[22]

In 1948, the Universal Declaration of Human Rights upheld previous rights. It established the right of equality and brotherhood among men, freedom and security, the right to life, and the right to privacy in their home and private life.

In 1964, the Declaration of Helsinki followed the tradition of maintaining established rights, establishing others to apply moral principles in research.

In 1966, the International Covenant on Civil and Political Rights dealt with people's rights, establishing that the State must protect the individual against discrimination; that is, professionals cannot make meaning of patients because of color, race, etc. when seeking it in their private practice or public office.

In 1975, the Declaration of Helsinki II brought the institution of the Ethics Commission for Biomedical Research in Human Beings, creating integrity safeguards to the physical and mental set of the patient, constituting the current concept of health.[23]

---

[21]KFOURI NETO, Miguel. **Medical Liability**. 4th ed.. Sao Paulo. Ed. RT, p.43 - 44, 2000.
[22]Radicchi, Ronaldo. **Civil and Criminal Liability of Dental Care to HIV-positive Patients.** 2001. Thesis (Master's degree in Dentistry) - School of Dentistry, State University of Campinas, Piracicaba, p. 82.
[23]Radicchi, Ronaldo. **Civil and Criminal Liability of Dental Care to HIV-positive Patients.** 2001. Thesis (Master's degree in Dentistry) - School of Dentistry, State University of Campinas, Piracicaba, p. 85.

In 1989, the Declaration of Helsinki IV addressed, among other topics, the civil and ethical imputability of physicians in research work, responsibility for the result always attributed to the physician, prevalence of the patient's interests over those of science and society, respect for the integrity and privacy of the patient and recognition of the possibility of damage to physical integrity, mental health and personality of the patient.

1.2 Brazilian legislation

With the arrival of the Portuguese in Brazil, we were subject to their legislation, initially in force of the Alfonsine Ordination (1446), and then were replaced by the Manueline Ordination in 1514.[24]

Subsequently, they were replaced by the Philippine Ordination, and even after Brazil's independence, they continued to take effect. It was only on the occasion of the first Brazilian Constitution, granted in 1824 by Emperor D. Pedro I, that Brazil organized itself as an independent nation.[25]

The Constitution of 1824 does not comment on the protection of dental treatment in a specific way.

In Brazil, the ancestral history of civil liability – or obligation to redress damages has its initial milestone in the Ordination of the Kingdom, denomination given to the Afonsino, Manueline, Sebastiânico, and Filipino Codes. In them, the influence of Roman law remained strong, which was expressly mentioned as a subsidiary source of positive law.[26]

Civil liability was linked to criminal liability, and there was a duty of satisfaction in the Criminal Code of the Empire due to the damage caused. However, it was not the dominant thought, and the defining element was the type of interest reached: public or private. In your

---

[24] PIERANGELI, José Henrique – **Penal codes of Brazil: historical evolution** - 2.ed. - São Paulo: Editora Revista dos Tribunais, 2001, p. 51-54.
[25] *Ibid.*, p. 65.
[26] PIERANGELI, José Henrique – **Penal codes of Brazil: historical evolution** - 2.ed. - São Paulo: Editora Revista dos Tribunais, p.54, 2001.

arts. 301 and 302 prohibited the covert use of any title, under imprisonment from 10 to 60 days and a fine, but were not strictly complied with, being the dental practice exercised for a long time by enslaved people, blacks, and mulattos.[27]

Câmara Souza, says in this regard[28]:

> The next phase, the third, begins with the genius of Teixeira de Freitas, who disagreed that civil liability was linked to criminal liability. He observed, in his writings, that the compensation for the injury caused by the crime was now addressed as competence of civil legislation. This occurred, according to him, as a result of the Law of December 3, 1841, having derogated from the Criminal Code, having revoked art. 31 and § 5 of Art. 269 of the Code of Procedure. At the same time, therefore, the institute of civil liability is consolidated as independent of criminal responsibility, also starting to be based on the concept of guilt, developing the theory of indirect responsibility, and admitting the presumption of guilt in the damage caused by inanimate things. At the same time, the principle of the burden of civil servants is developed.

Marilise Kostelnaki Chest, says: [29]

> In Brazil-Cologne, the Ordination of the Kingdom determined the obligation to satisfy the damage, according to Valler, when mentioning Art. 21, which dealt with the responsibility of the delinquent to repair the damage caused by the offense. Article 22 was determined to maintain that satisfaction should be as broad as possible and that, in case of doubt, the interpretation was made in favor of the offended. Article 29, in turn, dealt with the obligation of the heirs of the delinquent to satisfy the damage up to the limit of the inherited property. Until the beginning of the century, civil liability in Brazil concerning the public official was provided for in the Federal Constitution. The transportation of things was established in the Commercial Code. Specific law first appeared in 1912, dealing with the regulation of the liability of railways. The guiding principle, generic, on Aquilian responsibility, came with articles 159 and 160 of the Civil Code of 1916. From these rules emanate all other obligations of reservation of damages.

He began to consider non-compliance with obligations as non-compliance with legal texts and non-compliance with the contractual standard.

---

[27]VIANNA, Amílcar W. History of Dentistry in Brazil. In: OLIVEIRA, Marcelo **L.L.Dental Civil Liability.** Belo Horizonte:Del Rey, p. 34, 1999.

[28] SOUZA, Néri Tadeu Câmara . Available in:<http://www.conjur.uol.com.br/textos/17106> P. 01. Accessed August 30, 2003.

[29]Chest, Marilise Kostelnaki. **The health care contract and civil liability**. Ed. Forensic. Sao Paulo, 2. ed., p. 11, 2001.

In the Constitution of 1891, at the time of the Proclamation of the Republic, specific protection for dental treatment or the patient is not also mentioned.

In the Federal Constitution of 1934, Article 5, XIX, k, says: "It is privately incumbent on the Union to legislate on: conditions of capacity for the exercise of liberated and technical-scientific professions...]. "

And in art. 138, f, says:

> It is up to the Union, the States, and the Municipalities, to follow the respective laws: adopt legislative and administrative measures to restrict infant mortality and morbidity; and social hygiene, which prevents the spread of infectious diseases.

In turn, the Federal Constitution of 1937 brings in its article 16, XXVII: "It is privately incumbent on the Union to legislate on the following matters: fundamental norms of defense and protection of health, especially the child's health."

Here reference was made to health and its protection in our country. However, we observed that the Constitutions spoke little about fitness.

The following Constitution of 1946 also refers to the protection of health but does not deal directly yet with the profession of the dentist. This Federal Constitution, in its articles 5, XV "b" and "p," says: b) "It is up to the Union: to legislate on: general norms of financial law; social; defense and health protection; and scheme [...] " and p) "capacity conditions for the exercise of the technical-scientific and liberal professions."

The 1967 Constitution and Constitutional Amendment No. 1 of 1969 deal generally with health, containing three related articles. In this Federal Constitution, Art. 8, XVII, "c" and "r" say: "It is up to the Union to legislate on: general rules of financial law; insurance and social security; protection of health," and in the letter "r": "[...] conditions for the exercise of the liberal and technical-scientific professions."

Article 150, § 23, says: "The constitution ensures, ...] in the following terms: The exercise of any work, office or profession under the conditions of capacity established by law is free."

Article 158, XV, says: "The Constitution guarantees workers the following rights:[...] to improve their social condition: preventive health, hospital and medical care." [30] Here we see the concern for preventive health.

The man has been concerned about the aesthetic appearance and, as it could not fail to be, our smile was the cause of many concerns. Technological advances have occurred in dentistry, in the art of restoring dental functionality and aesthetics, either by the most efficient therapeutic techniques or by the most modern dental materials and equipment. Science has increased the expectation of oral health.

Nevertheless, as Miguel Kfouri Neto warns, the more present becomes civil responsibility in our lives as society evolves. Victims seek redress in cash to indemnify injury or compensate for death, reduced working capacity, pain, humiliation, or sadness.

1.2.1 The Federal Constitution of 1988

In the 1988 Constitution, health has a much more excellent treatment and its due importance. Moreover, it expresses the guidelines for citizens' rights.

In Article 5, the fundamental right to the protection of the person by the State in its non-economic aspect is expressed. In item III, it emphasizes that no one will suffer another mite or degrading treatment, still protecting the honor and image of people in its x item, being assured the reparation for material and moral damages.

It was greatly influenced by the international human rights landscape provided for in the Universal Declaration of Human Rights and the International Covenant on Civil and Political Rights.

Article 3, IV says: "They are fundamental objectives of the Federative Republic of Brazil: IV - the promotion of the good of all without discrimination of origin, race, sex, color, age and any other forms of discrimination."

---

[30] CUNHA, Alexandre Sanches. **All Brazilian constitutions.** Campinas: Bookseller, 2001.

Article 4, II says: "The Federative Republic of Brazil is governed in its international relations by the following principles: II – prevalence of human rights."

In Article 6, title II, which deals with Fundamental Rights and Guarantees, in Chapter II of Social Rights, the Constitution de 1988 says that they are social rights: education, health, work, leisure, security, social security, protection of motherhood and childhood, assistance to the needy, in the form of this Constitution.

Article 194 of Title VII, which deals with the social order within Chapter II of Social Security, defines Social Security as an integrated set of actions of the initiative of public authorities and society aimed at ensuring rights related to health, social security, and social assistance.

The Federal Constitution, in Title VIII, Chapter II, Section II, says about health in its art. 196: "Health is the right of all and the duty of the State, guaranteed through social and economic policies aimed at reducing the risk of disease and other injuries and equal universal access to actions and services for its promotion, protection, and recovery.

It establishes that health is everyone's right and the duty of the State. In his art. 197, he says:

> Health actions and services are of public relevance, and it is up to the Government to have, following the law, on its regulation, supervision, and control. Its execution must be done directly or through third parties and also by a natural or legal person under private law.

There is also the participation of the private sector. The private sector is given to complement the performance of the Unified Health System (SUS), being specific, however, that preference should be given to philanthropic and non-profit entities. In the same vein of ideas, the allocation of public funds for aid or grants to private for-profit institutions is forbidden. Similarly, the participation of foreign capital in health care in the country is defected, except through donations from international organizations linked to the United Nations, technical cooperation, and financing and loans.[31]

---

[31] BRAZIL. Constitution (1988). **Constitution of the Federative Republic of Brazil**. Brasília, DF: art. 199, § 3º

In its rendering, the SUS to which Art . 198 refers. It consists of an integration of public health actions and services, with guidelines for principle of decentralization, at the level of each sphere of government, integral service and community participation.

Article 200, II determined that health and epidemiological surveillance actions and workers' health are the responsibility of the SUS. "[32]

It enjoys numerous competencies in art—200, ranging from the control and supervision of procedures to collaboration in protecting the environment. Accordingly, laws No. 8,080 of September 19, 1990, and 8,142 of December 28, 1990, discipline the matter.

The Constitution of the Federative Republic of Brazil, in its article 6, relates health between social rights; in Art. 23, II, it assigns the Union, states, the Federal District, and municipalities competence to take care of public health, as well as to adopt measures aimed at ensuring protection for people with disabilities. To the cities, Art. 30, VII assigns competence to provide public health care services in technical and financial cooperation of the Union and the State. Finally, art. 200 establishes the competence of the SUS.

Health is conceived as the right of all and the duty of the State, which must guarantee it through social and economic policies aimed at reducing the risk of diseases and other injuries.

Health actions and services are of public relevance, so they are entirely subject to the regulation, supervision, and control of the Public Power under the law, which is responsible for executing them indirectly or by third parties, individuals, or legal entities of private law.

The SUS builds how the Public Power fulfills its duty in the legal relationship of health that has any person and the community in its active pole.

The Public Power is responsible for health actions and services, but health care can be done by the private initiative, whose institutions can participate in complementary to the SUS.[33]

---

[32] BRAZIL. Constitution (1988). **Constitution of the Federative Republic of Brasi** São Paulo.Ed. RT, 1996
[33] SILVA, José Afonso da . **Positive Constitutional Law Course.** Sao Paulo. Malheiros Editors. 13.ed, p.762, 1997.

1.2.2 The Civil Code

The Brasileiro Civil Code contains rules regarding the relations between individuals and the general (individuals in the sense that they are not agents or government agencies), including rules for compensation for damages in this relationship.

If the professional is a civil servant, Article 43 of the CC says: "Legal entities under domestic public law are civilly responsible for acts of their agents that in this capacity cause harm to third parties, with the right to regressive against the causes of the damage, if there is, on their part, guilt or deed."

Art. 389 of the CC states: "Without fulfilling the obligation, the debtor is liable for losses and damages, plus interest and monetary adjustment according to regularly established official indices, and attorney's fees."

In this case, the indemnification action occurs for damages caused by the delay in compliance with the established or controversial compliance manners, such as in the delays not provided for in the completion of treatments or the use of unspecified materials.

Article 935 comments that we cannot discuss the existence of the factor which was its author when these issues are already decided in criminal court.

Article 949 says: "In the event of injury or other offense to health, the offender will indemnify the offended of the costs of treatment and the lost profits until the convalescence, in addition to any other injury that the offended proves to have suffered."

In turn, Art. 950 says:

> If the offense is defective for which the offended cannot exercise his office or profession, or if he diminishes his ability to work, the indemnification, in addition to the costs of treatment and profits lost until the end of the recovery, will include a pension corresponding to the importance of the work for which he has become incarnate, or the depreciation he suffered— single paragraph. The injured, if you prefer, may require that the indemnity be arbitrated and paid at once.

It establishes the parameters for compensation for personal injury, creating the pension equivalent to the damage suffered due to the inability to work the offended.

Article 951 of the CC says that it should repay those who, in the exercise of their profession, cause harm or death by negligence, recklessness, or malpractice, not having a character as specific as had art. 1545 of the Civil Code of 1916, which had that doctors, surgeons, pharmacists, midwives, and dentists are obliged to satisfy the damage whenever recklessness, negligence, or malpractice in professional acts results in death, inability to serve, or injury.

Article 27 of the Consumer Protection Code says that the term is five years counted from the damage record and its authorship, but according to art. 206, § 3, V, CC, indemnification prescription of these actions occurs in 3 years.

1.2.3 The Code of Dental Ethics

The Dental Etha logical code was approved by CFO resolution No. 179 of December 19, 1991, and amended by Regulation No. 01 of 05.06.98. The text was based on the Final Report of the 1st National Conference on Dental Ethics, held in Vitória (ES), by the Federal Council and Regional Councils of Dentistry, in 1991. CFO resolution - 179/91.

When examining the Code of Dental Ethics, in article 1 of Chapter I, in the Preliminary Provisions, the following: "Art. 1. Code of Dental Ethics regulates the rights and duties of professionals and entities with registration in the Dentistry Councils, according to their specific attributions."

Article 1 referred to the objective of the Code of Ethics. In contrast, article 2 says: "Dentistry is a profession exercised, for the benefit of human health and the collectivity, without discrimination in any form or pretext."

This article addressed the importance of dental health for the general well-being of the human being, showing that oral health is of paramount importance for the concept of public health.

The professional should be aware of his duties and patients' rights and should also act according to the resolution of the Federal Council of Dentistry.

Art.3, I say: "They constrict fundamental rights of the dentist: to diagnose, plan and execute treatments, with freedom of conviction, within the limits of their attributions, observed the current state of science and its professional dignity."

It is concluded from this article that the professional should diagnose the problems and plan the treatments, including the presence of diseases such as AIDS and others that may manifest in the oral cavity.

The following article deals with the fundamental duties of the professional:

Art. 4. The fundamental duties of registered professionals are:

> I - to exercise the profession maintaining dignified behavior; II - to keep up to date on the professional and cultural knowledge necessary for the full performance of professional practice; III - to ensure the health and dignity of the patient; IV- to keep professional secrecy; V - promote collective health in the performance of their functions, positions, and citizenship, regardless of whether they practice the profession in the public or private sector; VI - prepare the clinical records of patients, keeping them in their file; VII - to point out flaws in the regulations and norms of the institutions in which they work, when it deems them unworthy for the practice of the profession or harmful to the patient and should address, in such cases, the competent bodies; VIII - advocate for harmony in class; IX - to refrain from the practice of acts that imply the commodification of dentistry or its miss interpretation;

> X - Take responsibility for the acts performed; XI - safeguard patient privacy throughout the service.

The Code of Ethics makes it very clear what is the purpose of Dentistry in its sixth article and refers to some care that must be taken in the professional/patient relationship: "It constitutes an ethical infraction: II – to avoid adequately clarifying the purposes, risks, costs and alternatives of treatment."

After investigating whether or not it is the professional's responsibility, it is of paramount importance to have all the documents such as budget form, anamnesis, radiographs, etc. To prove the costs arising from the treatment, it is necessary to keep them.

All forms of proof of the services provided to facilitate possible reconciliation of fees are essential in cases where the patient gives up treatment.

Thus, although it does not prevent judicial collection, the lack of a document signed by the patient may hinder it to the extent that the Court may arbitrate the lower amount in case of a challenge.

Following the Code of Dental Ethics analysis, in its ninth article, the care that the professional should have with professional secrecy will be treated.

Art. 9. It constitutes an ethical offense:

> I - Reveal, without just cause, a confidential fact that you know because of the exercise of your profession;
> II - Neglect in the guidance of its employees regarding professional secrecy.
>
> § 1. It is understood as a just cause, mainly:
> a) compulsory notification of illness;
> b) collaboration with justice in cases provided for by law;
> c) dental expertise at its exact limits;
> d) strict defense of the legitimate interest of registered professionals;
> e) disclosure of a confidential fact to the person responsible for the incapacitated.
>
> § 2. It does not constitute a breach of professional secrecy or the decline of the treatment undertaken in the judicial collection of professional fees.

The code deals with the arts. 16 to 18 regarding hospitalization, giving the dentist competence to:

> [...] internar e assistir o paciente em hospitais públicos e privados, com ou sem caráter filantrópico, respeitando as normas técnico-administrativas das

instituições. Estabelece como infração ética, no art. 18, executar intervenção cirúrgica fora do âmbito da odontologia, mesmo que em hospitais.

And among many issues, Article 36 deals with the penalties imposed and their applications: "The precepts of this Code are mandatory observance, and its violation will subject the infringer and who, in any case, with him compete for the infringement, the following penalties provided for in Article 17 of the Statute of July 10, 1998:

> I - reserved warning;
> II - public censorship;
> III - suspension of professional practice, up to one hundred and eighty (180) days, "*ad referendum*" of the Federal Council;
> IV - impeachment of the professional practice "ad referendum" of the Federal Council.

As we have seen, the Code of Dental Ethics is complete, ranging from the rights and duties of the dentist to the penalties to which they are subjected to the harmful practice of the profession.

1.2.4 The Consumer Protection Code

The Consumer Protection Code intended the objective responsibility of liberal professionals, forgetting the subjective element, but this was not received in the law's final text, and the responsibility of liberal professionals can only be ascertained by proving guilt.

The dentist is better able to provide the necessary evidence for procedural instruction because he has access to the clinical records and knowledge of the techniques required

For these reasons, in particular, situations, as provided for in the Consumer Protection Code, the judge may reverse the burden of proof by transferring to the dentist the task of proving that he acted without fault. In this case, it will be up to the patient only the burden of proving that a particular service was not provided as it should have been.

It constitutes an innovation in the relationship between the health professional and the public and private networks users. Article 3 defines the dentist as a supplier, whether as a natural or legal person, private or public, providing service in the health area.

Article 4 says that the patient is the consumer to whom the government's actions must protect due to their vulnerability to the market. It deals with Art. 6 of the protection of life, the right to information and education about treatment, prior clarifications on risks and damages, and protection against misleading advertising. It also has the right to redress property, moral, individual, collective, diffuse injuries, and free access to legal bodies.

Art. 7, sole paragraph; Article 25, paragraphs 1 and 2, and Article 34 deal with the case in which the dentist is employed, answering jointly and severally for the damage caused by his employee or product incorporated into the treatment.

The Consumer Protection Code (CDC) is an innovative law. After a few years in force (Law 8.078/90), brought the responsibility of the liberal professional in article 14, § 4, which says: "The personal responsibility of liberal professionals will be ascertained by verifying guilt."

This article establishes that the dentist will respond depending on the existence and proof of his guilt, and paragraph 4 personalizes his responsibility. Therefore, it was necessary that Paragraph 4 explicitly mentions this exception; that is, the personal responsibility of the liberal professional should be investigated as guilt, which is subjective.

The liberal professional should be understood as the one that the consumer *chooses intuitu personae,* where the elements of trust and competence are essential. When the liberal professional integrates a legal entity or provides services to him, their responsibility is objective. It cannot be discussed in personal responsibility, as mentioned in Article 14, § 4, of the CDC.

The CDC adopted the theory of risk for consumer relations, i.e., "...] the one who creates a risk to the consumer from his economic activity, to obtain profit, must indemnify the damages caused by the product or service object of this activity."

The need for proof of the fault of the liberal professional is an exception in the Consumer Protection Code, precisely because of the personal nature of the professional's services and the choice made by the consumer among professionals.

Cases may occur where the professional will respond objectively to the consumer, depending on the type of responsibility linked to the act; if it is an obligation of result, he will answer objectively and subjectively if it is a means. This subject will be dealt with in greater detail during the dissertation.

1.2.5 Federal and State health laws

Law 8,080 of 1990, The Unified Health System, regulates the activities of the SUS for public health actions in Brazil. It even governs the Private Health Care Network. Furthermore, it talks about individual guarantees, the establishment of regulations that standardize health actions, and their democratization.[34]

Articles 2 and articles and 3 and paragraph 3 and paragraph ensure the guarantees of the universality of services without discrimination.

The arts. 4th and 5th deal with the decentralization and participation of society in managing resources to democratize it.

Article 6 creates the Epidemiological and Sanitary Surveillance System and defines terms related to workers' health.

Article 7 and itis deals with the universality and equal access to health services, the integrity of this care, and the preservation of people's autonomy in defense of their physical and moral integrity.

---

[34] BRAZIL. 1990. Presidency of the Republic. Law No. 8,080 of 19/09/1990. **Organic Health Law.**

In art. 16, the competence of the SUS is given to developing standards for the control of working conditions and environment, in addition to others. In addition to the Union, the States, Federal Districts, and Municipalities also received the competence to develop technical guidelines for health surveillance.

Due to this law regulating the national health service, provided for in articles 20 to 23 and articles, the operating conditions are subject to permits issued after inspection of the establishments.

Due to these attributions, state biosafety standards were created, dealing with various attributions, including structural ones for the operation of public and private dental establishments, going from art. 22 to 32 and other articles, as mentioned in Annex D.[35]

The dental professional also has the responsibility to notify the Ministry of Health diseases, as stated by Law 8.080 of 09/19/90 that created the SUS in Brazil.

Art 8 says:

> Every citizen must communicate to the local health authority the occurrence of a proven or presumed infectious disease case, being mandatory for physicians and other health professionals and those responsible for public and private organizations and establishments of notification of suspected or confirmed cases of related diseases.

At the State level, health codes were created, defining responsibilities in cases of the need for notification, and biosafety standards, among other attributions. The professional can be held civilly and criminally liable throughout the country's territory.

1.2.6 No Criminal Code

The dentist's activity requires the handling of instruments that can cause lesions in the oral cavity of patients. When performing surgeries, for example, it acts injuring the oral tissues, but the Penal Code does not punish this "aggression" because it is a therapeutic purpose and the patient's consent.

---

[35] SÃO PAULO (State). Office of the Secretary of Health. **Resolution SS-15 of** 18/01/1999.

Criminal laws include norms that are more linked to the health profession and prohibit the illegal exercise of dentistry and practices such as charlatanism; deal with the omission of relief; abandonment of patients.

In addition to these norms, of a more general nature, are those that punish minor, serious, and severe bodily injuries.

Although initially not explicitly created for dentists, these criminal norms can often be applied to them in cases of dental error or situations in which the professional's performance, medication, or procedures may fall within one of the typifications of the Criminal Statute.

It is interesting to note that, in the case of a criminal conviction, manslaughter, or serious bodily injury, for example, the obligation to repay the victim or his heirs becomes automatic. Therefore, any further discussion in the Civil Court will be only about the amount of *indemnity (quantum debeatur)* and not whether or not it is due (*a debeatur*). These are the civil effects of the criminal sentence, as article 63 of the CPP says: "After the conviction, the sentence may be carried out, may promote the execution, in civil court, for reparation for the damage, the offended, its legal representative or its heirs."

In the case of an absolutory criminal sentence, for lack of evidence about authorship, facts, or existence of proof, the indemnification action can analyze all existing matters.

Although dentists are not mentioned directly in the articles of the Penal Code (PC), it is understood that being a professional, their responsibility is implicit in these articles (arts. 18, 121, paragraphs 3 and 4 and 129, § 6, in cases of negligence, malpractice, and recklessness).

Acting the dentist with guilt and if the result of this procedure is disability, weakness, disability, disuse of limb, sense or function, death, or abortion, will answer criminally for its act, without prejudice to repair the damage in the civil area. We can cite the loss of a superior permanent central incisor or the paresthesia of the facial nerve.

If you apply an anesthetic or take an X-ray, the dentist causes the abortion or causes harm to the fetus will answer for its actions. The able patient must declare in writing not to be pregnant.

The dentist must have a robust manual ability to manipulate sharp instruments and rotating instruments that can accidentally cause severe damage to the tissue structures of the oral cavity.

To exemplify types of lesions, we have, for example, an accidental cut in the surrounding soft tissues, the performance of an extraction that causes a fracture, or even significant loss of alveolar bone tissue and the intrusion of dental root into the maxillary sinus. In any of the three examples, the dentist will be in progress in criminal law. The Medical-Legal Institutes will define, after an accurate examination of the patient-body examination

1.2.6 No Criminal Code

The dentist's activity requires the handling of instruments that can cause lesions in the oral cavity of patients. When performing surgeries, for example, it acts injuring the oral tissues, but the Penal Code does not punish this "aggression" because it is a therapeutic purpose and the patient's consent.

Criminal laws include norms that are more linked to the health profession and prohibit the illegal exercise of dentistry and practices such as charlatanism; deal with the omission of relief; abandonment of patients.

In addition to these norms, of a more general nature, are those that punish minor, serious, and severe bodily injuries.

Although initially not explicitly created for dentists, these criminal norms can often be applied to them in cases of dental error or situations in which the professional's performance, medication, or procedures may fall within one of the typifications of the Criminal Statute.

It is interesting to note that, in the case of a criminal conviction, manslaughter, or serious bodily injury, for example, the obligation to repay the victim or his heirs becomes automatic. Therefore, any further discussion in the Civil Court will be only about the amount of *indemnity (quantum debeatur)* and not whether or not it is due (*a debeatur*). These are the civil effects of the criminal sentence, as article 63 of the CPP says: "After the conviction, the sentence may be carried out, may promote the execution, in civil court, for reparation for the damage, the offended, its legal representative or its heirs."

In the case of an absolutory criminal sentence, for lack of evidence about authorship, facts, or existence of signs, the indemnification action can analyze all existing matters.

Of crime - if there was a causal link between the physical damage recorded and the professional act- to characterize the guilt for malpractice, recklessness, or negligence.

Among the crimes that the dentist can commit in the practice of the profession is the omission of help, intentional bodily injury, guilt, and homicide.

Art. 135 of the CP says: "Failure to assist, where possible without personal risk to the abandoned or misplaced child, or to the invalid or injured person, to helpless or in severe and imminent danger: or not to ask in such cases for the help of the public authority. "

There may be the omission of help by the dentist in many situations in the various dental specialties. The most common are: to stop attending to a patient who underwent surgery and has to bleed in the postoperative period; to stop measuring a patient with severe infection due to surgical, endodontic treatment, etc.; to stop referring to a patient who presented an anaphylactic reaction after undergoing anesthesia in the emergency room or using his office equipment for cases of anaphylactic shock.

Suppose the patient turns to another professional and is treated, even though they did not result from the omission of help. In that case, they may take action against the professional who was unjustifiably omitted.

Concerning culpable injuries, lesions of oral nerves such as the lower alveolar in wisdom tooth or third molar extractions occur in the various specialties, resulting in implant softening scum or muscles; infections resulting in severe conditions; infections resulting from poorly performed endodontic treatments; prostheses that cause constant trauma; ingestion of toxic substances in the office; aspiration of endodontic files, etc.

Injuries may be caused accidentally, called culpable (art. 129, § 6, CP), or the professional may act intentionally, wanting to harm the patient, causing the so-called intentional injuries (art. 129, caput).

Death is more challenging due to dental treatments and may be due to a bodily injury (art. 129, § 3-Bodily injury followed by the end) or manslaughter (art. 121, CP). Maybe the result of anaphylactic shock by anesthesia or cardiac or hemorrhagic complications during treatment in patients presenting poor overall health. It will be ascertained whether the professional made a correct anamnesis in this case. Se acted prudently and will not be held responsible. Otherwise, it will be included in the articles of the Penal Code.

Law No. 9,099 of September 25, 1995, created the Special Criminal Courts to establish conciliation, trial, and execution of criminal offenses of lesser offensive potential, transferring conciliation, trial, and execution of cases to its sphere of jurisdiction of minor bodily injury and culpable bodily injury.

This possibility of conciliation mitigates the sentence of the dentist who is denounced for bodily injury because, to resolve conflicts by mediation and the compensation of the damage suffered by the patient, the professional will not suffer the custodial sentence if there is conciliation.

If there is an agreement and reparation of the damage, there is the renunciation of the right of representation of the patient and the filing of the process. However, even if there is no conciliation, the Public Prosecutor's Office may propose the suspension of the proceedings, where the judge will determine the necessary conditions to be fulfilled during the suspension.

1.3 The dental professional

At the beginning of the 16th century, Dentistry practiced in Brazil was rudimentary, restricted to dental extractions. The barbers, bleeders, and toothless worked, albeit without a license under the jurisdiction of the Chief Surgeon. However, the Royal Charter of October 25, 1448, promulgated by Don Afonso, King of Portugal, provided that no one could exercise the arts of physics and surgery without a special license issued by the Chief Surgeon.[36]

The first legislation in Brazil was the regulation of May 9, 1743. It was with this law that Tiradentes was authorized to exercise his office.

In the beginning, the practice of dentistry was rejected by doctors, falling into the hands of barbers and bleeders, often from the lower layers of society or even enslaved people and black ex-slaves.[37]

---

[36] ROSENTHAL, Elias. **Dentistry in Brazil. It's** history. Sao Paulo. Available in: <http://www.geocities.com/odontoufpr/historia.html>. Accessed August 15, 2003, p. 01.

[37] LERMAN, Salvador. History of dentistry and its legal practice. *In*: OLIVEIRA, Marcelo L.L. **Dental Civil**

On May 22, 1832, a decree was issued by Minister Lino Coutinho ordering the arrest and processing of all barbers and bleeders who illegally exercised dentistry.[38]

On September 29, 1851, a decree was issued in Brazil that disciplined dentistry as a health profession and could only be exercised with a license permit.

On October 25, 1884, Decree No. 9,311 annexed the dentistry course to medical courses in Brazil. During the Empire, illegal exercise was regarded as exemption, being a crime in the Penal Code of the Republic, 156 of the Penal Code,(Decree no. 847 of October 11, 1890).[39]

Law No. 3,141 of October 30, 1882, Art. 1, ended:

> Each of the Faculty of Medicine of the Empire will be named after the city in which it has a seat; be governed by a director and the Congregation of lenses, and will commit a course of medical and surgical sciences and three attached studies: pharmacy, obstetrics and gynecology and dentistry.

On November 15, 1921, Federal Decree No. 15,003 allowed the exercise of the profession of dentist to those who were qualified to be entitled to a title conferred by the faculties of Medicine officers or equivalent in the form of the law; graduates of foreign schools who qualified before national colleges or foreign professors with permission from the National Department of Public Health.[40]

For a greater understanding of the text, a definition of the person of the dental professional is necessary. This is a liberal professional, thus understood by Gabriel Saad[41] "...] who underpay, undertakes to provide a certain service for which he must to have certain technical and scientific conditions to serve the contracting consumer, without the proper subordination of employment relationships."

Liability. Belo Horizonte: Del Rey, p. 30, 1999.
[38]OLIVEIRA, Marcelo **L.L.Dental Civil Liability.** Belo Horizonte:Del Rey, p.34, 1999.
[39] *Ibidem*, p. 35.
[40] *Ibid.*, p.37.
[41] Saad, Eduardo Gabriel(**Consolidation of The Laws of Work Commented**. Sao Paulo. Ed. Ltr. 29 ed., art. 507, p. 383, 1996.

The professional practice of Medicine, Dentistry, and Veterinary Medicine and the professions of the pharmacist, midwife, and nurse in Brazil were regulated by Decree 20,981 of January 11, 1932. Still, in 1951, through Law No. 1,314/51, the exercise of dentistry was individualized to holders of a diploma recognized by the Ministry of Education and Culture.

Law No. 4,324, of April 14, 1964, dealt with the structuring of the Federal Council of Dentistry and the Regional Councils of Dentistry, attributing to each of the legal personality of public law as municipalities enjoying administrative and financial autonomy.

Under article 2 of the law mentioned above, the attributions of the councils have a supervisory function over the ethical behavior of professionals. They are responsible for the role of judges and disciplinarians of the dental class, caring and working, by all means at their fingertips, by the perfect ethical performance of dentistry, by the prestige and sound concept of the profession, and those who exercise it legally.

Law No. 5,081 of 08.24.66 governs the Regulation of the profession of dental surgeon in Brazil with specific standards. Acts against the regulatory rules entail penalties that will be applied by the class body, after administrative proceedings, according to the severity of the infringement. The penalties applicable range from censorship to the impeachment of the right to pursue the profession.

By this law, dentistry is autonomous, not being considered part of medicine, but its responsibility lies in the same plan, as shown in art. 951 of the CC mentioned above. It delimits the dentist's competence in article 6, which is in full in Annex "b" at the end of the work. This article exemplifies the professional's field of action, although it does not limit it.

Only in his ix item, he says: "[...] use in the exercise of the function of dentist auditor, in cases of necropsy, the access routes of the neck and head", cites a ban.

Legal norms are expressed through laws. Therefore, it is in the law that we must seek the rules of conduct made mandatory by the force of the law, and we will identify them in the various laws, in addition to the Constitution, already mentioned above.

2 CIVIL LIABILITY

The dentist should be aware of the importance of understanding its relationship with the law, what a skill is, and how it should be prepared with the necessary documentation.

For this reason, it has increased the courses of guidance to professionals offered by the organs of the class, that is, by the Association of Dentists of São Paulo, through its branches.

Art. 186 of the CC says: "He who, by action or voluntary omission, negligence or recklessness, violates the right and causes harm to others, even if exclusively moral, commits an unlawful act." This article deals with the obligation to repay on the part of those who, by action or voluntary omission, negligence, recklessness, or malpractice, has caused harm to others.

In addition to the fact that guilt must be characterized, the principle of proper causality must be in place, that is, that which considers as the cause of the damage only the act capable of producing it; one that is independent of the other would have been sufficient to make it unlike the theory of equivalence of conditions, where any circumstances that have run for the result would cause.

All are responsible for the conduct that would lead, by the expected unfolding of the facts, to that harmful result, entrusting the author with the burden of demonstrating it; also, on the injured, it is the burden of objectively proving that the necessary care was not provided, with the damage coming. This understanding is not peaceful.[42]

---

[42] BIERWAGEN, Monica Yoshiza. **Brief comments on causal link in multiple causality events**. São Paulo, 2002. Available from: <http:// www.editoraforense.com.br> Access on 10 Oct 2002, p. 01.

The professional knows that part of his treatments is destined to failure, especially in cases as extreme as the endodontic, when the dental structure is already significantly compromised, or in the case of mandibular and maxillary trauma surgeries. A dental error may also occur.

Elementary senses of law help the professional understand what dental error is and its legal, civil, and criminal consequences. For example, as a dental error, the fact that causes physical or psychic damage to a patient is considered the result of a guilty attitude of the dentist.

In addition to, guilt, which is an act without intent to harm, can happen with an intentional attitude, that is, with the deliberate and conscious will of the professional to violate the legal norm. This culpable act will characterize the obligation to repay.

The Regional Councils of Dentistry are organs established by Law 4,324 of April 14, 1964, responsible for the trial and punishment of the cirurgiões- dentists with professional practice. They have, however, administrative and disciplinary competence and cannot compel the dentist to repay the victim for his mistake. Executive deliberation, however, is compelling evidence to be used in judicial proceedings.

2.1 Concept

It is being responsible means answering for your deeds. Responsibility is linked to obligation, but it complements a more profound notion of duty. It follows from the acts of man in the face of this duty.

In the dentist's civil liability, the original cause is to restore the legal balance undone by injury or damage, recomposing the previous condition or delivering financial redress to the victim.[43]

---

[43]CALVIELLI, Ida T.P. The Consumer Protection Code and the Dentist as a Service Provider. *In*: SILVA, M. **Compendium of Legal Dentistry**. Sao Paulo. Medsi, p. 389,1997.

In Brazil, civil liability establishes that those who cause harm to others must repay them. The dentist's civil liability originates from this standard. The patient, suffering losses, can be compensated, whether the material damage or not.

We will talk about some concepts necessary to understand this legal situation between the professional and the patient. Concepts such as that personal responsibility and objective responsibility; contractual and non-contractual relationship, obligation of means, and obligation of income.

The man to live in society needs a set of rules. The law exists so that it becomes possible to live together. . This set of rules must be observed throughout the community, being an essential condition for its existence.

The Public Power organizes a territory politically, establishing a set of norms for the coexistence of society. The order is confirmed by the obligation to comply with the people's rules of a territory.

These rules must be obeyed by society, being aware that their non-compliance will result in sanctions, but not always the infringer of the law of compulsory conduct spontaneously accepts and complies with the penalties imposed on it for the violation of such a rule.

There are the proper mechanisms for the punishments to be applied. It is up to the judges to say the right to include the infringer in the corresponding article and must determine: whether the conduct attributed to the alleged infringer is lawful or unlawful; if there is evidence that the alleged offender effectively practiced the conduct contrary to the rules and among the punishments provided for in the law, which is the most appropriate.

Therefore, when the offenders do not spontaneously accept to carry out the conduct provided for in the mandatory rules or do not accept to comply with the penalties resulting from the violation of the laws, the judges, through a regular legal process, ascertain the facts, and on them, apply the legal rule applicable to the specific case, with due punishment.

It is up to the organs of the judiciary (judges or courts) before a dental error to ask and answer whether the fact constitutes a dental error if there is evidence, the extent of the damage, and the amount of compensation.

2.2 Subjective and objective responsibility

Silvio Rodrigues comments on the differences between the two types of responsibility: "Strictly speaking, it cannot be said that they are different species of responsibility, but other ways of facing the obligation to repair the damage. "[44]

To understand the difference between the types of liability, it is necessary to verify the existence or not of guilt and the type of obligation existing: obligation of result or obligation of means, which will be dealt with later.

A guilty act characterizes personal responsibility. Dental guilt is a deviation from a specific rule under which injury is observed. In addition to the indemnity act of the causative agent of the damage and the causal link present, there is also the fault of the causative agent of the damage. It is characterized by the presence in the act of this deceit or by the company only of guilt in the strict sense, that is, of recklessness, negligence, or malpractice.

The Code of Dental Ethics talks about the need to be qualified in art. 38, V, and the individual who acts as a dentist without complying with it may answer for recklessness or malpractice.

Often the patient seeking aesthetic or restorative treatment is already psychologically weakened, hoping to rescue all the frustration that time has brought him due to a bad appearance or, for example, a lousy dental or occlusal aesthetic.

Thus, in this case, the obligation of the professional assumes the twofold character of medium and result. In the means, because for its proper execution, it is necessary the diligent conduct of the dentist is sent to satisfy the final expectation of the patient. As a result,

---
[44] RODRIGUES, Silvio. Civil law. V.4. **Civil liability.** 18. ed. São Paulo: Saraiva, p.11, 2001.

considering that the debtor, in this case, the dentist, undertakes to perform, in favor of the creditor, who is the patient, a specific provision intended to obtain a concrete result, which is his dental aesthetic embellishment.

Nowadays, it is sought to preserve the dental element to the maximum, only if extracting in the last case, if there are no more resources or if the patient cannot do a more expensive treatment or go to a specialist.

When it occurs that an anterior tooth is affected in such a way that it requires endodontic treatment and the professional tries to save the tooth but mistakenly pierces it, compromising the success of the treatment, causing possible pain and a future loss of the dental element, the responsibility of the dentist becomes a mean and result.

A smile is the person's calling card, especially when looking for a job and in a relationship and accepted in the social environment. It must have a perfect aesthetic, which is highlighted by the significant increase in orthodontic treatments. They are people of all ages and not only children and adolescents from various professional fields seeking aesthetics or preservation of dental elements.

Currently, the dentist is not sought only to relieve pain. In addition to the search for harmony with orthodontic treatment, it is pursued with bleaching, porcelain veneers, aesthetic restorations, etc., to return the beneficial aspect that the dentition presented before dental involvement. In all situations, however, there is a contractual obligation. Despite having to stick or spend the tooth for endodontic treatment, for example, after the intervention, the dentist must proceed to aesthetic restoration of the lesion. Given this reality, the dentist's obligation is an obligation of means and result.

Some authors understand that when the dentist's obligation is characterized by having to achieve a result, it is objective responsibility. The objective responsibility is that there is no need to talk about guilt in which they act, the damage, and the causal link. It's based on risk theory. When the professional puts the patient in a risky situation and comes to cause him harm, he is obliged to repair it.

Article 927, the sole paragraph, gives an objective account of liability, which reads: "There shall be an obligation to repair the damage, regardless of guilt, in the cases specified by law, or where the activity normally carried out by the perpetrator of the damage implies, by its nature, the risk to the rights of others."

The objectivist civil liability was employed in the Romano Law, being deficient in the concept of guilt. Some authors understand that Lei Aquília provided for a particular subjectivity, a precursor to the theory of guilt.[45]

We believe that even in these cases, an analysis of the specific matter should be made because the dentist, for example, in the case of endodontic treatment of a superior anterior incisor, has the responsibility to save such an essential phonetic tooth and aesthetically, several biological factors such as pre-existing diseases and infections, the patient who does not collaborate taking the drug at the correct times and many other factors can lead to treatment failure.

According to Ida T.P.Calvielli,[46] the nature of the contractual obligation of dental services has been understood as an obligation of result, and compliance with the CDC would not be up to dentists to verify guilt since the responsibility would be objective. However, this position is not unanimous since the doctrine of the CDC is incompatible with the system of personal responsibility with guilt, which is the general rule of the Civil Code in its art. 186 and, especially, the art. Nine-five.[47]

---

[45] DIAS, José de Aguiar. **Civil liability**. 6. Ed. Rio de Janeiro: Forensics, 2v.,1979.
[46] CALVIELLI, I.T.P. **The Illegal Exercise of Dentistry in Brasil**. 1993 . Thesis (Master of Law) - Law School, University of São Paulo, São Paulo.
[47] NERY JR., Nelson. **The general principles of the Consumer Protection Code. Consumer Law**. Ed. RT.,3v, 44-77, 1992.

Thomasius and Heinnecius were precursors in the idea that the cause of harm should be held accountable, even without acting with guilt. On the other hand, Caio Mário considers the damage an objective reality, and one should not resort to the will to define civil liability.[48][49]

Maria Helena Diniz understands that objective responsibility is based on the beginning of equity, which comes from Romano Law; the one who profits from a situation must answer for the risk or disadvantages caused.[50]

Marcelo Oliveira says that[51]: "[...] contrary to what many authors claim, the dentist's obligation is not always a result", citing oral-maxillofacial surgery and traumatology as an example of a means obligation when the theory of personal responsibility is then applied. It also suggests the reform of § 4 of Art. 14 of the Code of Defense of the Consumer to: "[....] except when the consumer is obliged to achieve a certain result and this promise is the main furniture of the choice of the professional by the consumer", as a means of restraining doubts that arise.

2.3 Contractual and extracontractual liability

The contractual relationship is based on the autonomy of the will of the people involved. It is a convention between the parties, becoming law between them whatever is agreed.

Contractual civil liability originates from non-compliance with a contract, written or verbal. The effects of contractual liability are provided for in Article 389, CC: "The obligation

---

[48] OLIVEIRA, Marcelo L.L. **Dental Civil Liability**. Belo Horizonte: Del Rey, p. 55, 1999.
[49] PEREIRA, Caio Mário da Silva. **Civil law institutions.** Ed. Forensic. Rio de Janeiro, p. 16, 1996.
[50] DINIZ, Maria Helena. **Brazilian civil law course**. 9 ed. São Paulo: Saraiva, v. III, p. 42, 1994.
[51] OLIVEIRA, Marcelo L.L. **Dental Liability: Belo Horizonte**: Del Rey, p. 83, 2000.

has not been fulfilled, the debtor is liable for losses and damages, plus interest and monetary adjustment according to regularly established official indices, and attorney's fees."

Non-contractual or Aquilina liability is established by law and does not depend on the parties' will. Arising out of an unlawful act. The arts. 186 and 927 of the CC, already mentioned, speak of this accountability. In non-contractual liability is the patient who has to prove the professional's fault.

The contract is the act resulting from the agreement of wills between two or more persons on a specific and particular subject. It can be an agreement in which one person gives one thing and in return receives another (obligation to provide); it can also be an agreement in which one person undertakes to do something for the benefit of another (obligation to do), or finally, it may be an agreement by which someone undertakes not to do something for the benefit of others (duty not to do).

Furthermore, when it comes to the agents, they must be in the same capacity; that is, they must fully enjoy their physical and mental faculties so that they can validly manifest their will regarding the agreement that the contract ends.

Hence, it is essential when, in the dental treatment of children or adolescents under 18 years of age, they are accompanied by their parents or have authorized in writing that the professional acts. The dentist should also be aware of this detail and start the treatment. A responsible person must also sign the patient's anamnesis sheet over 18 years of age. As for the object, it must be lawful, permitted, or not prohibited by law.

When the clauses are pre-established, the contract is of a do-it-up. Most of the time, contracts establish reciprocal rights and obligations. In the purchase and sale, the buyer should pay the price and the right to the thing subject to the agreement; the seller must deliver the item to the buyer and the right to receive the amount corresponding to the adjusted price.

The clause of not indemnification in dental contracts is much discussed. Many believe that this is a null clause because it is contrary to the social interest. However, article 51, I of the Consumer Protection Code says:

> The contractual clauses relating to the supply of products and services that: I – make impossible, exonerate, or attenuate the supplier's responsibility for defects of any kind of products and services are null and void or make it impossible to express or attenuate the supplier's responsibility for defects of any products and services or imply waiver or provision rights. Indemnification may be limited in justifiable situations in consumer relations between the supplier and the consumer–legal entity.

This same article allows the limitation of indemnification liability, as cited when it is justifiable and the case of the consumer being a legal entity. No clause restricting or exonerating the duty to indemnify does not persevere about the natural person.

In professional contracts, most of the time, we are faced with an obligation to do or provide a service in which the contractor must use all his knowledge and skill to perform the work desired by the contractor.

Contracts for the performance of professional work can be: contracts in which the obligation is an obligation of result, such as the implementation of restorations considering fulfilling whether the desired purpose of the contractor has been achieved, such as when the contractor undertakes to use all means at their power, to achieve the objectives set forth herein, or the obligation of means, as is the typical case of the treatment contract endodontic by which, although the dentist cannot fully guarantee the recovery of the patient's injured tooth, assumes the obligation to put in the service the best technique or refer it to a specialist with more incredible experience, according to the concrete case.

By referring your patients to another specialist, we understand that if the professional acted according to the technique and if he made everything possible, proven through documentation, coming to the dental element to be lost, in the case of endodontic treatment, the professional is disqualified from responsibility, in cases where the dental part already has its structure significantly compromised, with the presence of cysts and long-standing infection.

According to Venosa, the dentist's responsibility is usually contractual by its very nature[52]. Although in the service contract, whether written or verbal, dentists undertake to provide more comprehensive services, including positive results, and many factors interfere with the success of dental treatment. External factors include asepsis in the place where treatment is being performed, such as an office or operating room, medications, or even the patient's reaction.

Middle contracts are the most frequent. In the middle are the work of restorations, dental prevention, and other day-to-day treatments of the dental office.

That is why, in the vast majority of cases, under the contract, the dentist is not obliged to restore the oral health of the patient because dentistry itself is not an exact science. Still, it is obliged to develop its professional activities, conducting itself with those attributes required of every responsible professional, namely: attention, care, and diligence in the application of the knowledge of his art, to achieve the goal of restoring or restoring the oral health of the patient, within the limit of what is possible.

In professional contracts, most of the time, we are faced with an obligation to do or provide a service in which the contractor must use all his knowledge and skill to perform the work desired by the contractor.

When a natural or legal person provides the service, there is also a difference. When a clinic gives it, for example, the established relationship is contractual. Therefore, they respond according to what is written in the contract, not being necessary if proven guilty, but only the default. This is because, in this case, the CDC has an application.

---

[52]VENOSA, Silvio de Salvo. **Civil law: civil liability.** 3 rd ed. São Paulo: Atlas, p. 107, 2003.

In this case, it was not the professional's conditions, such as knowledge, skill, and prestige, that led the patient to hire, answering the clinic regardless of guilt. So now, when the dentist divides the profits and expenses in the clinic, he will answer only the dentist who performed the treatment without losing his character.

This does not occur with non-contractual liability, which is derived from the norms of life in society and not from a contract, like most relationships between dentists.

2.4 Medium and resulting bonds

Middle obligations are those where the professional has a personal responsibility, not committing to achieve a result. It must employ the contractor all his diligence and be prudent, using the techniques adopted in the profession. You will only respond if the patient proves his guilt in case of damage. In this case, the professional acts without guaranteeing the result.

For Maria Helena Diniz, a means obligation is when the debtor undertakes to use ordinary prudence and diligence in providing a particular service to achieve a result without being bound to obtain it.[53]

The result obligations occur when the professional has an objective responsibility, committing to achieve the desired result. If you do not reach the result, even if you have acted competently, you will have to repay because the obligation of result generates an objective responsibility, assuming your guilt if you do not reach the desired end.

The contractor undertakes to achieve a delimited objective, a particular result, to satisfy what was required by the contractor.

---

[53] DINIZ, Maria Helena. **Brazilian civil law course**. 9. ed. São Paulo: Saraiva, v. II, p. 157-158, 1994.

Demogue was the first to make this classification between means and result. He understood that the obligation of means requires nothing more from the debtor but the use of the means known for a given purpose and those of development, which the person is obliged to achieve the desired result. Outside contracts, there would only be medium obligations.[54]

The dentist works to solve a physical suffering (means obligation) and aesthetically repair the patient's dentition (result obligation). We believe that because it depends on a biological response, dental services should be considered, at first, as mean obligations. However, some authors understand the responsibility of the dentist is more of a duty of result, even if they know that it will not always be a result.[55]

Studies are needed to verify the probability of a treatment reaching 100% success in concrete cases. It is often difficult to know whether an obligation is mean or result. It may be that a therapy that today is considered a medium due to technological advances is a result in the future.

The form of hiring and the physical possibility of achieving the desired result should be considered. If the contractor is obliged to achieve a result, and this was the determining reason for the performance of the contract, the obligation is a result.[56]

Ida Calvielli says that these promises currently occur from rudimentary forms, such as the most sophisticated, ensuring services even in writing.[57]

The dentist cannot take advantage of the form of hiring to remove their responsibility, even if they have a term signed by the patient.

Nelson Nery Jr., concerning the responsibility of the liberal professional, states:[58]

> A distinction must also be made between the obligations of the medium and those of the result so that the responsibility of the liberal professional is perfectly characterized. When the duty of the liberal professional, *even if*

---

[54] DEMOGUE, René. ***Traité des obligations in general*** apud KFOURI NETO, Miguel. **Medical guilt and burden of proof.** São Paulo : Editora Revista dos Tribunais, p. 227, 2002.
[55] VENOSA, Silvio de Salvo. **Civil law: civil liability.** 3 rd ed. São Paulo: Atlas, p. 107, 2003
[56] OLIVEIRA, Marcelo L.L. **Dental Civil Liability**. Belo Horizonte: Del Rey, p. 73, 2000.
[57] CALVIELLI, Ida T.P. Professional responsibility of the dentist. In: SILVA, Miguel. **Compendium of legal dentistry**. São Paulo: Medsi, 1997.
[58] NERY JUNIOR. The general principles of the Brazilian consumer protection code. São Paulo, v.3, p. 44-77, 1992.

chosen intuitu personae by the consumer, is of result, his responsibility for the accident of consumption or service addiction is objective. In reverse, when it comes to a means obligation, § 4 of Art. 14 of the CDC applies in its entirety, and the professional's responsibility should be examined under the theory of guilt. In any case, in the actions of indemnification filed in the face of the liberal professional, whether it is an obligation of medium or result (objective or subjective), it is possible to inversion the burden of proof in favor of the consumer, as proclaimed by Art. 6, VII, of the Code.

To know if the obligation is medium or result, says Marcelo Leal de Lima Oliveira, [59]" [...] it is necessary to observe two things: the form of hiring and the physical possibility of achieving the useful result of the contracted obligation."

Oliveira divided the obligations of medium and result of the dentist according to his specialty. However, it is worth mentioning that each case deserves attention and may undergo modifications in the concrete case, especially if the professional commits to the result.

SPECIALTY	OBLIGATIONAL NATURE
Restorative dentistry	Result
Orthodontics	Result
Oral pathology	Result
Dental	Result
Dentistry in public health	Result
Radiology	Result
Endodontics	Result
Oral-Maxillofacial Traumatology Surgery	Middle
Legal Dentistry	Result and a half

---

[59] OLIVEIRA, Marcelo L.L. **Dental Civil Liability.** Belo Horizonte: Del Rey, p. 73, 2000.

Pediatric dentistry	Result and a half
Periodontics	Result and a half
Maxillo Facial Prosthesis	Result and a half
Stomatology	Result and a half
Implantodontia	Result and a half

Kfouri Neto[60] also understands the following specialties as an obligation: endodontics, periodontics, pediatric dentistry, and oral-maxillofacial traumatology, among others depending on the specific case. We believe that endodontics should be classified as a means obligation, as this author points out.

The obligation can also result when the professional makes a promise, ensuring that the treatment will be in a certain way, such as before and after shown in computer programs.

2.5 The civil liability of the dentist

Previously, the dentist's responsibility was subjective, contractual, and predominantly medium. SilvioVenosa also agrees with the predominance of contractual liability but understands it more strongly as an obligation of result and may be of means.[61]

It is subjective because the dentist to be held accountable in the event of a dental error depends on the proof of having acted with guilt in the exercise of his profession.

In the Civil Code art. 951 says:

> The provisions of the arts. 948,949 and 950 also apply in the case of compensation due to the one who, in the exercise of professional activity, for negligence, recklessness, or malpractice, causes the patient's death, aggravates the evil, causes injury, or inability him to work.

---

[60] KFOURI NETO, Miguel. **Civil liability of the doctor**. 3 rd ed. São Paulo: Revista dos Tribunais, p.211, 1998.
[61] VENOSA, Silvio de Salvo. **Civil law: civil liability.** 3 rd ed. São Paulo: Atlas, p. 107, 2003

In these articles, the Code clears the so-called personal responsibility in which there is a need for the characterization of guilt (negligence, recklessness, and malpractice) so that compensation is attributed to the offender of the damage.

It is contractual because, at the time of the budget that the professional gives to the patient, both establish a contractual relationship, resulting from the agreement of wills, regarding a service provided by the professional.

The patient participates by paying for the services and receiving treatment in return. This characterizes a contractual relationship, provided that the object is lawful and the agents are capable and not prescribed by law.

The obligation can be medium, result, or medium according to the specialty, which will be better explained below. According to the subjective theory adopted by our Civil Code, in the arts. 186 and 951, it is up to the victim to prove the officer's fault or guilt for further reparation for the damage suffered.

Often the proof is difficult. But, in some cases, it admits objective responsibility or responsibility without guilt.

One cannot identify different responsibility species in these concepts[62] but different ways of seeing the obligation to repair the damage. Responsibility inspired by the idea of guilt is subjective and objective when illuminated by the idea of risk.

I was considering the nature of the contractual obligation of the dental surgeon's services, having been understood. As a result, it could be interpreted that in the case of a complaint against the service provided, the verification of guilt would not be necessary.

As Nery points out,[63] "[...], a distinction must also be made between medium and result in obligations, so that the responsibility of the liberal professional is perfectly characterized. [...] The formula to resolve the issue is to conduct a prior examination to determine whether the professional's obligation is of medium or result.

---

[62] RODRIGUES, Silvio. **Civil Law**. Vol II. Ed. Saraiva, São Paulo, 2001
[63] NERY JUNIOR. The general principles of the Brazilian consumer protection code. São Paulo, v.3, p. 44-77, 1992.

Those who see guilt as a fundamental element of civil liability say that guilt has a moral foundation and, therefore, responsibility cannot be conceived but for it. The human being is responsible for repairing an act of his own and the damage he has caused.

Many have opposed the idea of guilt as the foundation of civil liability, seeking to aim at this concept. The human being is a biological being and not exact; many factors lead to succession or failure of treatment. You have to see

Statistically, what are the chances of treatment being successful or not and how the patient's cooperation can influence this outcome?

There are limits to the dentist's performance and can perform in the office or outpatient clinic surgeries that require only local anesthesia and within dental specialties, which according to Article 39 of Resolution 185/93, are: surgery and oral-maxillofacial traumatology, restorative dentistry, endodontics, legal dentistry, collective health dentistry, pediatric dentistry, orthodontics, oral pathology, periodontics, oral-maxillofacial prosthesis, dental prosthesis, radiology, implant, and stomatology.

The professional is also responsible when an employer, as provided in Art. 932, CC, for the acts of his employees and those placed in the exercise of their work. Summary 341 of the Supreme Court (STF) also says: "It is presumed the fault of the employer or principal for the wrongful act of the employee or representative."

This Summary confirms the dentist's responsibility for acts of third parties that work directly under his responsibility. You may be free from guilt if you prove that you did *not act with "in iligendo"* guilt for safely choosing a representative and not failing to supervise your acts (culpa *in vigiling*). If the responsibility is objective, there will be accountability.

Since the dentist is the final responsible, when auxiliary professionals are reliable such as prosthesis technicians, oral hygiene technicians, dental office attendants, and dental prosthesis assistants, they will be able to respond jointly. They may have the right of return against these aides. [64]

3 SPECIES OF GUILT

In this chapter, we will address the species of guilt and their relationship with civil liability in cases of dental errors. Guilt can be conceptualized as failure to observe a duty that the agent should know and watch.

Days [65] conceptualizes guilt as:

> The fault is a lack of diligence in the observance of the norm of conduct, that is, the contempt, on the part of the agent, of the effort necessary to observe it, with an unintended result but foreseeable, provided that the agent destines the possible consequences of his attitude.

Culpability in the civil field is divided into intentional and not intentional. There is a significant difference between both because the action aims at a calculated result in the deed, while in guilt, the step is due to negligence, malpractice, or recklessness. Brazilian Civil Law has elected guilt as a center of personal responsibility that guides civil liability in its art. 186 (CC).

Guilt is divided into three degrees in traditional doctrine: severe, light, and very light. The grave crudely manifests itself, approaching the deed. It includes conscious guilt, where the agent assumes the risk that the event could happen. Mild guilt is characterized by violating a duty of conduct relating to the average man in situations where he would not transgress the duty of conduct. The very light guilt is seen by the lack of occasional attention, which only someone with special knowledge could have. The amount of the damage establishes the damage and not the degree of guilt.[66]

---

[64] VENOSA, Silvio de Salvo. **Civil law: civil liability.** 3 rd ed. São Paulo: Atlas, p. 108, 2003.

[65] DIAS, José de Aguiar. **Civil liability**. 6. Ed. Rio de Janeiro. Ed. Forensic. 1v, p. 136, 1979.
[66] VENOSA, Salvo's Ílvio. **Civil law: civil liability**. 3. Ed. São Paulo: Atlas, p. 25, 2003.

3.1 Civil liability with culpa

The fault consists in the deviation of an ideal model of conduct, represented, sometimes by good faith, others by the diligence of the good father of the family (*pater familias*). The Code of Napoleon established the beginnings of guilt as the source of the duty to indemnify and said in art. 1,382: "Every human fact that produces the damage of another person obliges the one for whose fault this occurred to repair it." Art. 1,383 said: "Each one is liable for the damage due to his act and his negligence or recklessness."[67]

The individual in society must be attentive to the reality of social interaction, avoiding practices that may, in any way, cause harm to others.

The concept of guilt is not just the abstention from doing something forbidden. However, also, when the individual in society is compelled to act, to perform some activity, it will be necessary to do so considering the rules or techniques inherent to it, as well as employing his attention and care in any action or task from which it may potentially result in danger to the life, health or property of others.

The idea of the dentist answering through guilt predominates in the doctrine, regardless of the absence of a contract, because the obligation to repair the damage will always exist, inside or outside the contract.

The dentist will only be held responsible if he no longer fulfills his duties of informing and advising, assisting, and prudence.

---

[67] OLIVEIRA, Marcelo L.L. **Dental Civil Liability:** Belo Horizonte: Del Rey, p. 45, 2000.

This duty consists, initially, in the correct professional performance, in the need for him to establish with his patient the conditions of payment, the services to

Agreements it serves, the price of the consultation, etc., the duty to inform and advise.

At this stage, the dentist should explain the treatment proposed thoroughly to the patient and the state of the oral elements and structures, alerting him of the risks of his specialty so that the patient is fully informed.

It also consists of the provision of the services contracted in the best possible way, answering the calls, and trying to keep informed of the patient's health conditions during treatment, the duty to assist. In emergency cases, the professional should be easily found so that abandonment is not characterized and leads to accountability.[68]

You can stop seeing the patient but never abandon him, taking into account that this refusal does not cause immediate harm and should communicate what happened to the patient or a relative.

This duty to assist and prudence belongs, among other things, to the way of acting of the dentist. Innovative treatments, not recognized by dental science, can be made, or involve significant risks, without the authorization of the patient or their family members when the patient is unconscious, as in the case of trauma, where the oral-maxillofacial surgeon must act promptly.

The fault is still characterized if the dentist does not act prudently. It can represent recklessness, acting carelessly, negligence if it ceases to adopt the appropriate measures, or malpractice, by non-compliance with the technical norms of the profession. [69]

---

[68]CHABAS, François. . The responsibility of the doctor for damage caused in the exercise of the profession, in the right French. Riv. Responsabilità Civile e Previdenza, Milano: Giuffrè, anno 1988, vol. LIII apud KFOURI NETO. **Culpa Médica and Ônus da Prova.** Ed. RT. 2002

[69] SILVA, M.S. **Compendium of Legal Dentistry** : Ed. Medical and Scientific Ltda. São Paulo,1997.

The dentist doesn't want to miss it. Through his studies in undergraduate and graduate courses, he assumes that he can work in various specialties.

The dental error occurs when, despite not intending, it causes physical or psychic damage to the patient. This act is characterized by the lack of intent, or deed, being a guilty act.

Today, with so many specialties and solutions to almost all problems in the oral universe, the professional feels the need to expand his knowledge and cannot venture to work in implantology or extensive surgeries without qualification.

Ideally, each dentist would have a specialty and leave for improvement constantly. It is a risk to think that as a general practitioner, you may be able to act in all specialties correctly, acting with all techniques, although it is possible.

One of the problems preventing this position is the high costs of dental courses and the low value of market competition regarding the various treatments.

The professional has to be well qualified, take costly courses, and can not charge a reasonable price to cover the expenses of the material and techniques due to the low prices exercised by the competition.

Professional errors can be divided, according to Lutz[70], into:

> 1º Errors and Accidents in Anesthesia: a certain percentage of deaths and accidents occur in anesthesia, especially in general anesthesia;
> 2nd Diagnostic errors: A. Per action: a) examination done with defective technique; b) erroneous interpretation of semiological data, although correctly obtained. B. By default: lack of the use of an indispensable resource, such as radiography.
> 3º Treatment errors: A. Per action: a) choice of improper treatment; b) use of inadequate instruments and contraindicated, dangerous, or exchanged remedies, a lousy technique in interventions or the prosthesis laboratory, including in the manufacture of orthodontic appliances. B. By default: for example, the lack of treatment of infected canals or bleeding, lack of root extraction before the placement of a total prosthesis, lack of indispensable advice.

---

[70] Lutz, Adolpho Gualter. **Errors and Accidents in Dentistry**. Rio de Janeiro. Ed. Est. From Arts Graph, p. 50-51,1938.

4º Errors of prognosis: These errors give less opportunity to a process, and these errors must result in appreciable damage.

5º Falta de higiene: por exemplo, o contágio e transmissão de doenças como a sífilis à boca do cliente pelas mãos do cirurgião-dentista etc.

6º Errors nas perícias.

France[71] teaches:

> "[...] the dental error in the field of responsibility can be of a personal or structural order. It is personal when the harmful act occurred in action or omission due to technical and intellectual unpreparedness, gross dismay, or occasional reasons related to physical or emotional conditions. It can also come from structural failures when the means or working conditions are insufficient or ineffective for a satisfactory response."

The use of inadequate equipment can cause the failure of the professional and their unpreparedness or carelessness. Unfortunately, it is not uncommon in Brazil to come across poorly equipped offices or more than twenty or thirty years of service.

For example: when the sugar does not work or does not have the correct ability to keep the surgical field free of saliva, it can compromise the preparation of restorations or in the endodontic treatment, where it is also necessary to isolate the dental element from saliva, it can cause contamination of the canal since it has many bacteria.

When the faults are technical, they are classified as personal, and when they refer to the equipment, they are structural.

Currently, the office looks like a laboratory because there are so many devices present, or that must be, according to the specialization exercised, ranging from X-ray devices, ultrasound apparatus for removal of tartars, bicarbonate jet, greenhouses, light-curing machine, electric scalpel, dental laser, optical microscopy, and many others.

The professional is free from guilt if an error occurs not related to technical or structural failures, as in the case of unforeseeable accidents resulting from a fortuitous circumstance or major force. Being unforeseen, it could not be avoided.

Suppose the dental problem has a bad prognosis, such as reabsorbed canals or teeth with cysts or acute infection. In that case, the loss of the dental element arising from the very evolution of the disease does not hold the dentist responsible.

---

[71] FRANCE, Genival Veloso de. **Medical Law**. Sao Paulo. Byk Publishing Foundation. 6. ed., p. 242, 1994.

Dentists are charging popular prices, working outside ethics because due to a large number of patients, it is often not possible to sterilize material for the appropriate time. Another fact is the reuse of disposable materials such as gloves, suckers, etc.

France[72] teaches:

> "[...] the dental error in the field of responsibility can be of a personal or structural order. It is personal when the harmful act occurred due to inaction or omission due to technical and intellectual unpreparedness, gross dismay, or occasional reasons related to physical or emotional conditions. It can also come from structural failures when the means or working conditions are insufficient or ineffective for a satisfactory response."

The failure of the professionals and their unpreparedness or carelessness can be caused by the use of inadequate equipment. It is not uncommon in Brazil to come across poorly equipped offices or more than twenty or thirty years of service.

For example: when the sugar does not work or does not have the correct ability to keep the surgical field free of saliva, it can compromise the preparation of restorations or in the endodontic treatment, where it is also necessary to isolate the dental element from saliva, it can cause contamination of the canal since it has many bacteria.

When the faults are technical, they are classified as personal, and when they refer to the equipment, they are structural.

Currently, the office looks like a laboratory because there are so many devices present, or that must be, according to the specialization exercised, ranging from X-ray devices, ultrasound apparatus for removal of tartars, bicarbonate jet, greenhouses, light-curing device, electric scalpel, dental laser, optical microscopy, and many others.

The professional is free from guilt if an error occurs not related to technical or structural failures, as in the case of unforeseeable accidents resulting from a fortuitous circumstance or primary force. Being unforeseen, it could not be avoided.

---

[72] FRANCE, Genival Veloso de. **Medical Law**. Sao Paulo. Byk Publishing Foundation. 6. ed., p. 242, 1994.

If the dental problem has a bad prognosis, such as reabsorbed canals or teeth with cysts or acute infection, the loss of the dental element arising from the very evolution of the disease does not hold the dentist responsible.

Dentists are charging popular prices, working outside ethics, because due to a large number of patients, it is often not possible to sterilize material for the appropriate time. Another fact is the reuse of disposable materials such as gloves, suckers, etc.

Public services also commit these structural failures, with the scrapping of available dental equipment and lack of consumer material and instruments, with a real risk of contracting diseases such as AIDS and hepatitis B.

As a precaution, dentists in the State of São Paulo have been vaccinated against the most severe diseases. Among them are hepatitis B, tetanus, and diffrhyphtheria. Vaccination occurs to protect against the terrible effects of these diseases on professionals, as well as protection of patients.

Acting as public sector employees, if the dental error of one of these structural failures happens, the professional cannot be held responsible as long as he does not compete in the event.

If this is the case of compensation, the action should be directed against the municipal, state, federal district, or federal public agencies.

3.1.1 Negligence

It is negligent the professional who acts with careless, inattention. He omits, becomes inert, passive, and does not do what he should do according to good technique.

You may be held liable for negligence similarly, for letting third parties, such as helpers, and dentistry students without supervision, perform treatments on their responsibility.

Some dentists place the attendants or even the secretary to, for example, glue the brackets on the patients, in the case of orthodontics, and may lead to the unevenness of the teeth by placing them in the wrong position.

If it causes damage due to poor maintenance of your dental equipment, the dentist will also answer for negligence, as in the case of clogged suckers, lack of water in the high-rotation pens, burned reflector lights, etc.

Damage can happen in private practices, as well as in clinics and hospitals. Other examples are burns on the oral mucosa by drug substances, trauma due to falls of patients poorly positioned in the dental chair, forgetfulness of cotton inside the canal when performing the restoration, letting objects fall into the patient's pharynx, not controlling the postoperative period and not warning of the risks of treatment.

In prescription, errors of medications can occur from the mistake of the drug, indicating the wrong remedy, such as the exchange of the therapy, because the pharmacist does not understand the dentist's letter.

The professional should be attentive to all the signs and symptoms presented by the patients, using the tests and resources to give the correct diagnosis.

The lack of identification of abscesses, cysts, and oral wounds, and not giving the correct referral to the patient can cause severe damage.

In every profession, mistakes happen; this is man's nature, but the dentist has to work with the details as if he were a goldsmith in rebuilding a precious stone, which is the tooth.

Like pearls, teeth have a lot of value, and all seek to preserve them. So it is surprising that the professional can be responsible for the loss of the same by carelessness.

3.1.2 Recklessness

It is a hasty action, which puts the treatment at risk, skipping certain phases of treatment, such as the placement of dressing in the canal before the definitive filling, the lack of X-rays of the files, cones, endodontic treatment, or the appropriate gingival clearance for molding in the prosthesis, exposing the risk of treatment success.

In recklessness, the dentist acts without the necessary caution characterized by intempestivity and precipitation.

It is to act by which the agent, having the possibility of predicting a harmful event, does not do so, thus causing the dangerous occurrence. The predictability of the occurrence of the destructive event is characteristic of this culpable modality. He knows it can do damage. You're predicting the outcome, but you're trying to keep going.

Recklessness is distinguished from malpractice because while the professional decides to perform a treatment with a technique that does not dominate, it acts with malpractice. In recklessness, a slip occurs, a lack of care, such as performing restorations or surgeries without need.

It also acts recklessly for the professional who wants to perform the treatment quickly or with excessive force in tooth extraction, causing a jaw fracture.

3.1.3 Malpractice

The dentist acts with malpractice when performing procedures concerning which he does not have sufficient knowledge, does not master the technique, or does not have specialized preparation to perform the act. It also responds to malpractice when mishandling equipment, causing damage to the patient due to their malpractice in technique.

It has been questioned whether a dentist could be an expert to have a higher education degree recognized by the MEC. Professor José Luiz Gavião de Almeida understands that he can be unskilled mainly because the professional has a preparation (verbal information). There is also a collective responsibility.[73]

In the buccal-maxillofacial surgical team, the surgeon is the head of the group. Traditionally being the head of the team, he is responsible for the acts committed by any team member.

It may occur in anesthesia, where the professional should be at the patient's bedside. In addition, it occurs in various dental specialties such as: in surgery, when extracting a dental element causes a maxillary fracture; in implants, neural canal injury; in the prosthesis, the manufacture of a double or unitary total prosthesis with the vertical dimension changed to more or less, etc.

It is present in an emergency that occurs due to a high risk of life due to failure in the vital functions of the patient. These situations can happen in the office, on the street, or elsewhere and the professional should be prepared, preferably having an oxygen device in the office, especially for cases of death due to the application of anesthesia, which may occur due to the state health of the patient, or due to the psychological state, that is, the fear of the same, so that malpractice is not characterized.

Law No. 5081 of August 24, 1966, in article 6, which establishes the dentist's competence, item VIII provides: "it is up to the dentist to prescribe and apply urgent medication in the event of serious accidents that compromise the life and health of the patient."

In addition to knowledge of the technique, the professional must know pharmacology and physiology to understand the effects of prescribed medications. For example, you should

---

[73] Information obtained in the master classes of Civil Law of UNIP prof. José Luiz Gavião de Almeida, who very well observes that can only be imexpert who has professional training.

know the dose, the time between the ingestion of one and the other, the route of administration, whether it is oral or intramuscular, by injection.

There is a danger of combining remedies and undesirable collateral effects. Pode harms the health of the patient and even leads to death. The greatest threat is if the patient is allergic to any medication. Therefore, the initial anamnesis must be performed before starting any treatment.

Current computer programs highlight in red in these patients the condition of allergic and, if the traditional clinical record is made on paper, it should be highlighted.

Patients with heart problems, hypertension, diabetes, and many other diseases require special care: certain anesthetic for cardiac patients; people with diabetes should be compensated, etc.

A symptom that is rarely identified in advance and only appears at the time of treatment is the patient's psychological state, which can contribute to the failure of treatment. For example, this state can be during the time of the effect of the anesthetic, passing the result faster in the more nervous patients.

It can happen from bleeding and must have the medication of its own and material to stop it until it reaches the fainting. Suppose the case is very severe and the use of oxygen is not sufficient to bring the patient to consciousness. In that case, the dentist should have an emergency ambulance service prepared to take the patient to a hospital.

This service is being offered to dentists in the State of São Paulo through a monthly contribution.

Careful acting is a way to avoid malpractice. In addition, it is a benefit for the patient and tranquility for professionals.

To ascertain the fault in malpractice, the judge should compare the procedures and care that should have been adopted in the specific case with that adopted by the dentist. If the criteria are not met, you will have acted with guilt.

It will be taken into account the attitude adopted by a prudent professional in that case, under the same circumstances, and there is a particular difficulty in proving guilt.

There are cases, such as in the preliminary endodontic treatment, which is done in a sterile way, with all the precautions that science requires. Depois on this dental element, another professional specialist, makes a prosthesis, which requires the inclusion of a nucleus inside the tooth.

It should be in mind that a careless act can contaminate the work done by the professional specialist in the canal and compromise the future of the dental element. In this case, whose responsibility would be if the tooth were to have endodontic problems again? How do you prove the guilt of one or the other?

Therefore, there is a need to have in the archive the radiographs and the other documents proving the use of good technique and, perhaps, the most sensible was the endodontics professional himself to prepare the cavity for future placement of the nucleus, that is, each specialist working within his field of activity.

Dental treatment usually happens without the presence of third parties, unless an assistant is present, but will have its testimony also compromised by the working relationship with the dentist. Even in a surgery team, it would be difficult for some professionals to testify against the other.

Add to this the fact that when it becomes necessary a dental expertise, it is performed by a colleague of profession, who may even be experiencing equal difficulty or simply want to "protect the class", which compromises impartiality. That's why the derogatory expression "white mafia" was attributed.

Judges can use other evidence when it is difficult to obtain the evidence, as in the example following Des's judgment delivered in the TJRS. Ruy Rosado de Aguiar Júnior judging appeal no. 589,069,996 of the 5th Chamber:

> I conclude the report on matters of a legal nature, outside the scope of my expertise. I regret that [...] omitting to answer about relevant questions, by merely formal aspects in the formulation of the question, and dogmatically

> answering others, as mainly occurred [...] Due to the deficiencies of this evidence, it was determined the diligence of leaves, so that the medical service, then sought by the author, sent the data recorded there about it. But, as is expected, it was not successful in the collection of enlightening reports; hence the need for a renewed attempt, equally frustrated,[...] What exists, however, is enough to judge the merits of the action.

As a rule, in Brazilian procedural law, the burden of proof rests with those who claim it. Therefore, the test would always be up to the patient or victim, who is often a person with fewer resources, more straightforward and without many studies, and may occur the reversal of the burden of proof, as mentioned by the Consumer Protection Code.

Hence the need for the dentist to make the prescription in two ways and make the patient sign that he is aware of his responsibility to take the medications at the correct times as a way to protect himself against malicious people who want to take advantage of the situation to be reimbursed for a fact to which they were responsible.

3.2 Dallure ducts

When the agent, voluntarily and consciously, practices the act contrary to the legal norms, by wanting the result of taking the risk of producing it. Ex: the professional, knowing that the patient is sensitive to penicillin, inoculates the product to kill him, is practicing intentional homicide; in the same situation is who, not understanding the reactional behavior of the patient, applies a penicillin injection to him without doing any previous sensitivity tests, assuming the risk of killing his patient and effectively does so. In the first hypothesis, we have the direct intent; in the second, the eventual deed.

3.3 Civil guilt, criminal and administrative guilt

Even if meanings of civil guilt and criminal guilt present distinctions, such as criminal guilt is characterized by its typicality, that is, prohibited conduct must be described in criminal law, which is not required of civil responsibility; while the Penal Law is paying the punishment, civil law is aimed at compensation; the penal is individual, while civil can be applied to other people.

In the course of the civil liability of the dentist, it is necessary to behave as own or his employees in the practice of the profession, taking the duty of care and technique must be by way of deed or guilt, and the causal link should be present.

Administrative guilt refers to the determination and punishment applied to the facts and professional acts of the dentist by the Regional Councils in which he was enrolled in the tempo of the fact or act liable to punishment. The penalties that the Regional Councils of Dentistry can impose range from censorship to the exclusion of the dentist from the condition.

The offenses can range from a simple disagreement with the patient treating him with lousy education, and may lead to criminal crimes, such as the case of crimes against honor: slander, defamation, or injury, provided for respectively in articles: 138, 139, and 140 of the PC, going up to crimes such as the omission of help, bodily injury, and homicide.

3.3.1 Lack of First Aid

When the professional falls into the crime of omission of aid, he will answer criminally by art. 135 of the CP, which says:

> Stop assisting, where possible, without personal risk, to the abandoned or lost child, or the invalid or injured person, to helpless or in severe and imminent danger; or not to ask, in such cases, for the help of the public authority.

The professional may answer for the omission of help when he no longer attends for no justified reason, a patient affected by a bleeding, a severe post-surgical infection, who will faint in the office and not provide immediate help; a patient who presents severe pain and is not medicated, etc.

Each case will be analyzed concretely, seeing the participation of both the dentist and the patient for the outbreak of the facts.

If convicted criminally, this sentence may be used for civil damages; it is the civil effects of the criminal punishment. Art 91, I of the CP, says: "These are the effects of the conviction: I – to make certain the obligation to indemnify the damage caused by the crime."

Concerning administrative effects, the dentist may suffer until the practice of the profession is revoked, in the last case, following Art 36, IV of the Code of Dental Ética.

If you are a civil servant, you may lose your position or function, as article 92 of the CP says: "These are also the effects of the conviction: I – the loss of office, civil service or elective mandate."

This penalty is applied when the professional is sentenced to a custodial sentence of one year or more, in case of abuse of authority, and four years, in other cases.

3.3.2 Corporal wounds

The acts performed by the professional may result in injuries of various forms, both in the oral tissues and in dental structures, and the dentist may be involved in the following articles of the Penal Code:

> Art. 129 – Penal Code: Offending the bodily integrity or health of others" - penalty: ten (3) months to one (1) year.
>
> Pair. 2. o – It turns out
>
> I - permanent incapacity for work
>
> II - an incurable disease
>
> III - loss or loss of limb, sense, or function
>
> IV - permanent deformity

V – abortion

>Penalty – imprisonment from 2 (two) to 8 (eight) years.
>
>Par.6º - If the injury is culpable:
>
>Penalty: detention from 2 (two) months to 1 (one) year."

In addition, the criminal conviction will still be subject to civil and administrative indemnity by the Regional Council of Dentistry, as mentioned earlier.

3.3.3 Murder

As previously treated, the culpable crime is characterized by the absence of deed and willingness to commit the crime. Still, there is the responsibility of the professional to be able to answer in the event of the death of the patient. Article 18 of the CP says: "It is said the crime:[...] II – culpable, when the agent gave cause to the result by recklessness, negligence or malpractice."

And Art. 121 of the Brasileiro Penal Code says in his caput: "Kill someone: Penalty: imprisonment from 6 (six) to 20 (twenty) years. "

Par. 4 says: "In manslaughter, the penalty is increased by a third if the crime results from non-observance of the rule of profession, art or craft. "

Although dentists are not mentioned directly in the articles of the Penal Code, it is understood that being a professional, their responsibility is implicit in these articles (arts. 18, 121, paragraphs 3 and 4 and 129, § 6) in cases of malpractice and recklessness.

Here you may also have to repay civilly and suffer administrative sanctions by the Regional Council of Dentistry. If you are a civil servant, be removed or lose your position or function.

3.3.4 Homicide with intention

In simple homicide, the professional acts to cause death to the patient, which seems to us more fiction than reality; even so, it would be in progress in article 121, CP, which says: "Killing someone: Pity – imprisonment, from 6(six) to 20 (twenty) years. "

It could occur in the case of injecting an anesthetic with penicillin, knowing that the patient was allergic to the drug.

In addition to criminal penalties, you would be subject to civil and administrative indemnities through the Code of Ethics and loss of office or function if you are a public official.

3.4 The causal relationship between the conduct and the old result

For the configuration of the dental error, there is a need for a causal link between the culpable action and the result, that is, a cause-and-effect relationship. So the harmful effect should be the result of the guilty action. The absence of the causal link between the activity of the dentist and the resulting damage removes the blame.

To identify whether the result can be attributed to a given action, it is not enough to eliminate the step to verify whether the effect would occur because this is the theory of equivalence of conditions and is very broad.

Damage and causal link have as a consequence indemnification civil liability, but it takes action or wrongful omission. The difficulty is usually here in the demonstration of the causal connection. It's the most extensive discussion in the courts.

So, we have as elements: the agent, the act that is the harmful result of an unlawful act, an unwanted effect, professional guilt, therefore, without the intention of harming. The actual, practical, and concrete damage, the causal link, when the act is performed

Unlawfully in moderation, without due attention, it is sometimes an accident, as in certain surgeries where there are risks.

Suppose a given patient would fatally die, in the manner and at the time he died, regardless of the action or omission of the dentist. In that case, no responsibility can be attributed to him because between the event of death and the act or omission of the professional; there was no causal link, or rather, the action or omission of the optional was not determinant for the cause of death of the patient.

Now, suppose by action or omission of the dentist, the patient died. In that case, he must be held responsible to the extent that the result of the death of the patient resulted from the action or omission of the professional. It is tough to have the end of a patient in dental treatment, and this happens more due to anaphylactic shock by anesthesia, or in the specialty of the oral-maxillofacial surgeon, where general anesthesia is used and also in cases where the professional works in hospitals, serving patients who are victims of trauma in accidents.

This causal relationship is established, as a rule, through expertise. This is because the judge lacks specific knowledge of areas foreign to The Right. For this reason, among the judge's assistants are the experts: people who produce reports (in the form of documents or reports) containing their reasoned opinions regarding technical facts due to their specific technical knowledge.

The causal link must present some characteristics, such as the existence of a temporal relation between the result and the act, a topographic relationship, proximity between the site of the lesion and that of the action, as well as a coherent relationship between the fact and the possible lesions that may occur, continuously, demonstrating that one is a consequence of the other, and an analysis of similar cases that resulted in the same injury.

Therefore, the great importance of expert reports that will verify, in concrete cases, the existence or not of a link between the conduct of the professional and the result of damage to the patient. One can conceptualize the causal relationship as the causal link between the culpable act performed by the professional and the production of the damage.

The profession of the dental surgeon is surrounded by norms of behavior that guide all activities. This normative set is composed of various laws and decrees, some general and others of a specific nature.

In the civil and criminal sphere, the general rules are the Civil Code and the Penal Code. Within the specific norm, essentially administrative and extrajudicial, are the provisions of the Federal Council and the Regional Councils of Dentistry and the Code of Dental Ethics (CFO Resolution No. 179, of 19.12.91).

3.5 Proof burden

As the dentist's responsibility is contractual, there is a presumption of his guilt, just proof of his default. In addition, however, there are obligations of medium and result and subjective and objective responsibility, as seen earlier.

We understand that the professional respond subjectively concerning the obligations of the environment, and, being his responsibility, it is necessary to characterize his guilt.

Evidence must be provided by both him and the patient, as the judge usually receives evidence from both parties. However, suppose it is the case that the professional does not want to give the proof of treatment, radiographs and other means of evidence. In that case, the judge may reverse the burden of evidence in favor of the patient, leaving the professional to deliver them. According to the point, if there is sufficient evidence, the judge may consider the patient's arguments genuine before the refusal the professional.

3.6 Exclusions of responsability

They are exclusions of responsibility, which prevent the existence of the causal link. As for the exclusion of liability, in the contractual field, we have the clause of not indemnify, by which the contracting party that would undertake to compensate them for future losses stipulates in the contract, agreeing with the contractors, the irresponsibility for default, not caused by you, but by a third party or force primary. [74]

This is the conventional dismissal of the duty to repair the damage, and the risks are transferred to the victim.

This clause is debatable and is not peacefully accepted in Brazilian jurisprudence. Many believe that this is a null clause, as it is in consumer rights (Art. 51, I). When the patient signs with the dentist a treatment, an obligation is born for the parties, with rights and duties for both.

Another example is the victim's guilt, where the cause-and-effect relationship between the damage and its cause disappears. Finally, we also have the unforeseen case, when something unexpected occurs superior to the will of man and, the force greater, that is, when if he knows that the fact will happen, but can not avoid it.

---

[74] SILVA, De Plácido and . **Legal Vocabulary**. Rio de Janeiro. Forensic Editor, 1998.

Other exclusions are the state of necessity, where there is justification for the harm caused to the victim due to an imminent evil, which on the imminence of seeing a right reached by him, offends others' rights. Self-defense, in which to repel unjust aggression, current or imminent, against you or others, can use the necessary means. The regular exercise of law, because it acts in the routine practice of a recognized right and the fact of a third party,

understood as someone other than the victim and the cause of the damage. They cannot be connected to the agent causing the damage. In the present case, it is necessary to ascertain whether the third party was the sole cause of the damage or whether the agent also competed for the damage. The concurrent fault is one of the partial exclusions, in which the responsibility is both the dentist and the patient.

There is both the professional's responsibility in the dental area and of the patient. To solve the conflict, one must analyze the concrete case and its facts, framing whether it is an obligation of medium or result.

The dentist is responsible for the damage caused to the patient due to defects in the equipment, restraining himself from this responsibility if he proves the occurrence of the lucky case, force greater force, guilt exclusive to the victim or no indemnification clause, getting the right of return against the equipment manufacturer. As an example, we can mention the patient who makes a sudden movement when using the high-rotation drill by the professional, causing injuries to his oral mucosa.

According to the specific case, the professional will also be guilt-free if the dental error occurs by the fortuitous case or force primary, as in the case of ending the energy in the region of the consultory, collapse, flood, etc.

3.7 The consent informed

The growth of lawsuits against dentists has contributed to distrust, especially complaints about the lack of information to give consent, that is, informed consent. There is now a severe problem that is information. In the United States, a doctor who does not have information can be held responsible. There needs to be a causal link between lack of knowledge and damage. There is a statistically relevant risk in specific procedures that are not warned to the patient (verbal information).[75]

Even using the best technique, necrosis, which is tissue death, can occur and has, as a consequence, failure in surgery. The doctor was expert, prudent, and considerate. And by no means negligent. He effectively caused the damage because you didn't tell the patient. As a result, the patient could refuse to undergo surgery.

The most common problem of lack of information occurs when the doctor gives the patient wrong information regarding the convalescence period and says that after surgery, in 15 days, the patient returns to his activities and spends a month or more, and the patient does not recover.

This is an erroneous procedure. Today in the United States, there is also a demand for excessive information. For example, a doctor gave a patient a notebook with 13 reports of the risks. The woman did not undergo surgery but panicked. These demands (verbal information) are already happening in Brazil.

Informed consent is not unless the doctor is given way, and when this documented burden is attributed to the doctor, this will result in their disfavor (verbal information)."

A woman who underwent dental treatment and then arrived home, her husband does not agree with the price or the treatment, may want to cancel the payment and, if the professional does not prove that the patient agreed, may be subject to a lawsuit.

---

[75] KFOURI NETO, Miguel. *In*: **SYMPOSIUM ON THE CIVIL AND CRIMINAL LIABILITY OF THE DOCTOR.** Campinas, São Paulo: 2002.

The professional must produce the document. This informed consent is a relationship of dialogue between patient and doctor and has been greatly important. In the future, it will occupy the interest of professionals' rights

4 AESTHETIC AND FUNCTIONAL DAMAGE

The damage is an injury to an interest done illegally and may allow compensation. These are interests that are unfairly affected. The damage or interest must be current and specific, not indemnify, in principle, hypothetical damages. It can be patrimonial or moral. It materializes with the definition of the injury suffered by the victim.[76]

While property damage is the resulting loss of property, decrease, or deterioration of material things, moral damage affects moral goods such as freedom, honor, profession, and family.

According to Silvio Venosa,[77] aesthetic damage is a mode of moral damage. It can be accumulated with property damage, such as decreased working capacity, but does not accumulate with moral damage, under penalty of encore *in idem.*

Concerning aesthetic treatment, this rule of personal responsibility changes a little. The patient does not need treatment or pain. For his vanity, he chooses to change his teeth' aesthetic appearance, place crowns or porcelain veneers, or make a dental whitening, for example. It's not emergency treatment.

---

[76] VENOSA, Salvo's Ílvio. **Civil Law: civil liability**. 3. Ed. São Paulo: Atlas, p. 28, 2003.
[77] *Ibid.*, p. 37

The dentist's goal is to satisfy the expected change of the patient, that is, the aesthetic improvement of the teeth of his client.

If the traffic is risky and the professional is unsure of the result, it is better not to throw yourself into this adventure. It would help if you informed the patient of the risks. Dental damage can cause consequences of patrimonial or moral order and aesthetic damage.

In emergency surgery, it is worth taking the risk to save the patient's life. In other cases, such as jaw reposition surgery, it is already an aesthetic treatment to correct bone growth deficiencies of the jaw, and the risk should be minimal.

Most jurists in Brazil understand that the result of cosmetic surgery is medium. Still, others differ from this opinion, as in cases of restorative surgeries performed by the oral-maxillofacial specialist.

Professor Luís Andorno, a professor at the National University of Rosario, who is currently in Porto Alegre, quoted the French jurist Professor François Chabas, sharing his [78] understanding, saying that according to Chabas, "[...] according to the conclusions of medical science of recent times, the behavior of human skin of fundamental importance in plastic surgery is unpredictable in many cases." For them, therefore, in cosmetic surgery, the doctor's responsibility would be in the middle.

This opinion is shared by Min. Ruy Rosado de Aguiar Jr., who wrote so (RT 718/33):

> However, the hit is with those who attribute the aesthetic surgeon as a means of obligation. Although it is said that plastic surgeons promise to correct, without which no one would undergo, being, to surgical intervention, so they would assume the obligation to achieve the promised result, the truth is that the ale is present in every surgical intervention and unpredictable the reactions of each organism to the aggression of the surgical act.

Marcelo Oliveira says that[79] "[...] contrary to what many authors claim, the dentist's obligation is not always a result", citing oral-maxillofacial surgery and traumatology as an

---

[78] CHABAS, François apud KFOURI NETO. **Medical guilt and burden of proof**. Ed. RT., p. 253-254, 2002.

example of a means obligation when the theory of personal responsibility is then applied.

It also suggests the reform of § 4 of Art. 14 of the Consumer Protection Code to "[...] unless it is obliged to achieve a particular result and this promise is the main furniture of the choice of the professional by the consumer," as a means of clarifying doubts that arise.

In case of bodily injury, the professional will repay the patient in the treatment expenses, with the emerging damage and lost profits, until the end of its recovery, with the debt updated monetarily.

Art. 949 of the CC says that the cause of the injury will indemnify the offended treatment expenses and lost profits until the end of the recovery and even another injury that the offender may have suffered.

You will also be entitled to the pension following Art. 950, CC, if the offended cannot exercise his office or profession or have their ability to work diminished and the costs of treatment and lost profits until the end of recovery.

The sole paragraph says that if the injured person prefers, they may demand that the indemnity be arbitrated and paid at once. The amount to be repaid will be fixed by aesthetic damage, considering several patient factors, such as age, place of injury, sex, profession, and all forms of damage.

Among some of the complications that can happen we have: post-extraction hemorrhages, the presence of pain and infections in endodontic treatments, the resorption of the roots in orthodontics, the breaking of files within the canals, cuts in the oral mucosa, burns by chemical or physical agents, etc.

Responsibility for sterilization of the material used may be charged if proven that it was not properly sterilized.

4.1 Orthodontics and ATM

---

[79] OLIVEIRA, Marcelo L.L. **Dental Liability: Belo Horizonte**: Del Rey, p. 83, 2000.

Orthodontic treatment aims to restore an ideal and stable aesthetic and physiological position for the teeth. Still, for this purpose, it can cause injuries or dysfunctions in the joint-temporomandibular (TMC).

The conditions on both sides of the face tend to adapt to where the jaw fits. However, trauma may occur without the patient noticing or presenting symptoms such as pain and clicking when opening and closing the mouth.

These traumas can also be caused by the ingestion of substantial snacks, where the patient has to open the mouth a lot, or continuous use of the gum.

Repetition in trauma can thus injure TMC, and surgical intervention is required to correct damaged structures.

TMD dysfunctions are usually followed by pain, and there may be jaw locking, where the patient can no longer close the mouth, as if "the chin had fallen."

Most orthodontic movements cause some root resorption. Therefore, the professional should be attentive to new techniques that use lighter forces to control and avoid this resorption. In addition, the loss of bone structure over time can lead to softening of the teeth.

The smile is an actual "business card" for the person when presenting in a new job or a social relationship. Hence the concern with orthodontic correction.

Root resorption happens more in adults. This is because the root surface has a thicker layer of cement and cementoblasts in a small number, in addition to many periodontal fibers attached to the root, which has, as a consequence, a more incredible anchorage, that is, the resistance of the dental element, avoiding its movement.[80]

Depending on the tooth, some have easier resorption than others. However, especially when the patient has very protracted teeth, that is, forward, to the point of not being able to close the lips, and their traction back can cause resorption in the upper incisors due to the great movement required.

---

[80]FREITAS, M.R. et al. **Orthodontic drive-review of the literature. Clinical considerations and presentation of a clinical case.** Ortod. V.18, n.2, Jul/Dec. 1985.

This movement can cause resorption, especially if it is an intrusive movement, that is, into the alveoli, where the tooth is lodged in the bone.

Besides presenting a certain resistance to movement, the adult has lower plasticity of the spongy bone.

The loss of part of the root by resorption will not always decrease the life of the tooth or its masticatory capacity. However, factors such as lack of personal hygiene due to poor brushing, causing tartar buildup, and causing inflammation of the gums and periodontal structure, are relevant to treatment success.

It is necessary to separate the responsibility of the orthodontist and what participation the patient may have in the event of a failure.

The orthodontist or the general dentist who makes orthodontics is responsible for controlling the resorption of the teeth and should put them in an appropriate aesthetic and functional position—fixing the crossbites, present when the teeth, instead of fit, the bottom ones inside the top, reverse the positions, which is a cause of trauma in the TMM. The median line of the upper and lower teeth should be aligned with the face.

Acting correctly, without using excessive forces and within the technique adopted, despite all care, can still, after the end of treatment, already in the phase of tooth containment. With the use of removable appliances, recurrence occurs; that is, the teeth return to warp.

There is a tendency for teeth to return to their original position due to factors such as the non-complete calcification of the bone that surrounds the root or a neuro-muscular memory that tends to exert a force on the tooth, causing it to move.

This adaptation is also physiological, where the occlusion of the upper and lower teeth seek a more comfortable position to perform chewing. The professional should be aware of all these factors to prevent the tooth from recidive.

In this post-treatment phase, the patient has a primary role. Depending on the correct use of containment devices, usually removable in the maxilla and fixed on the part of the mandibular teeth, glued internally from canine to canine, one will arrive at the success of the containment.

The treatment aims to reposition the teeth, leveling and aligning them. However, it cannot result in a more unstable positioning than before it started.

The courses of improvement and specialization are precisely for the dentist to qualify, not having to bear expenses in lawsuits and indemnification.

The truth is that the concern with stability should begin with the planning of the future position of dental elements and the possibility of recurrence. In the anamnesis, it should be asked if someone in the family, for example, has used the device and if recurrence occurred after treatment.

For more than once, it has already occurred in the practice of dental offices, cases of patients who sought the best specialists, and after finishing treatment, in the containment phase, the teeth began to warp again.

There is no consensus on how long it takes to make the restraint, varying wildly with the specific case.

Orthodontics recognizes that specific extractions are necessary to accommodate the remaining teeth to the space available in the dental arches. However, deciduous teeth or milk cannot be extracted before time to accommodate permanent teeth. There will be no room for the corresponding permanent forming under the extracted tooth.[81]

Treatment requires theoretical knowledge and good-quality appliances. The sooner you can start intervening in orthodontic problems, the better your prognosis.

Many general practitioners fail to diagnose serious occlusion problems such as crossbite or lack of jaw or jaw bone development. Therefore, it is necessary to begin the intervention in orthopedic issues (growth and positioning of the jaws) as soon as possible.

---

[81] Lutz, Adolpho Gualter. **Mistakes and accidents in dentistry**. Ed. Est. From Graph Arts. Junior C. Mendes. Rio de Janeiro, p.206, 1938.

There is a controversy about whether the general practitioner could act by placing orthodontic apparatus or not. The Federal Council of Dentistry (CFO) reaffirmed that the general clinician could perform the treatment, according to resolution 185/93. On the other hand, some jurists understand that only the specialist could act.

The professional can be held responsible for the failures in all the above-mentioned items.

4.2 Implants

In the various techniques used, after surgery to place the implant, it should be a while in place without exerting forces on it so that the osteointegration occurs, that is, the union of the implant with the bone.

After this period, the prosthesis will be placed on the implant to restore the masticatory function.

Many people seek to recover the missing teeth through the implants, restoring the aesthetics and masticatory function that have been lost over the years. There was an extractive policy, forming a country toothless in the past.

Buccelli[82] et al. did a work based on removals of implants motivated by problems of a clinical nature and by expert determination. They concluded that the most frequent cause of legally relevant error in this specialty would be not to show the patient contraindication cases.

The materials used in implants currently have almost no rejection, succeeding in about 90% because titanium is a nontoxic material.

---

[82]BUCELLI, C. et al. *Su alcuni casi di rimozioni obbliogata di implantoprotesi. Riflessioni clinique and dimplicazioni médico-legali*. Min. Stom. V.38, n.9, p. 105-109, 1988. *In*: FRANCE, Beatriz Helena Sottile. **Civil and Criminal Liability of the Dentist.** 1993.Thesis. (Master's degree in Legal Dentistry and Deontology) - State University of Campinas, Piracicaba, p. 42.

What causes failure with the consequent possibility of compensation is the placement of intra-bone implants at angles that cause future excess force applied by chewing, causing bone resorption, for example.

It may also be unsuccessful due to a lack of hygiene in the healing phase or poor application of the recommended technique. There are several techniques for the different types of implants, national or imported.

There is also the possibility of abscesses and exposure of implants to bacteria present in the oral cavity and saliva, leading to the loss of the implant. Usually, when this occurs, one can remove it and perform another implant in the same place after a healing time.

If there are failures in this process, from surgery to healing, the professional can be held accountable.

4.3 Dental prosthesis

Rene[83] et al. did a search in *the records of the Medical Responsibility Board and the National Board of Health and Welfare on* complaints of inadequate prosthetic treatments in Sweden and identified that the most frequent errors were: occlusion or vertical dimension; crowns lost or retained; extension errors; pain, inflammation; retention and adaptation errors; aesthetic mistakes.

The dental prosthesis can be fixed or movable, in whole or part. The so-called fixed porcelain or metal-plastic bridge depends, to achieve success, on the correct preparation in the various phases, ranging from the choice of the appropriate tray, gingival clearance, molding, and proper preparation of the core or tooth, and quality of the material, avoiding distortions.

---

[83]RENE, N.;O WALL, B. In: FRANCE, Beatriz Helena Sottile. **Civil and Criminal Liability of the Dentist,** 1993 Thesis (Master in Legal Dentistry and Deontology) - State University of Campinas, Piracicaba, p. 51.

Its correct adaptation following the patterns and curves of Spee and Monson will influence its success, not overloading the strong points of its structure because it may not occur with the continuous use and strength of chewing.

In the case of a mobile bridge, in addition to these observations, there is the possibility of causing damage to adjacent dental elements if the hooks are poorly made or generate instability, if the occlusion of the dental elements is not correct, and may cause pain in TMD or even fracture of the movable bridge.

In the total prosthesis, a. denture, the vertical dimension and muscle strength of the facial muscles should be respected and should be made in a size that does not cause injury in the gums, or if the tension points are not worn out, even excruciating wounds, which will cause a great constrain to the patient.

Michelis[84] evaluated dental lesions in civil liability, revealing the importance of the coefficient of antagonism on the possibility of the limits of prosthetic reintegration and the need for renewal of the prosthesis.

A poorly adapted prosthesis can cause lesions in the periodontium, in the structures around the tooth, due to the overload of forces coming from chewing.[85]

It is of paramount importance that the prosthesis respects the vertical dimension, fulfills its chewing function, and does not cause problems in TMC.

There may be losses of one or more fixed or removable bridge pillars. Care should be taken so those prosthesis elements such as crowns will not be aspirated by the patient and may even end up in the lungs, requiring future surgery for their removal.

The indications of unnecessary and inadequate treatments characterize the guilt and the lack of adaptation of the prosthesis in the dental arches.

---

[84]MICHELIS, B. In: FRANCE, Beatriz Helena Sottile. **Civil and Criminal Liability of the Dentist,** 1993. Thesis (Master's degree in Legal Dentistry and Deontology) - State University of Campinas. Piracicaba, p. 16.
[85]GIBILISCO, J.A. Resorption Processes. In: FRANCE, Beatriz Helena Sottile. **Civil and Criminal Liability of the Dentist,** 1993. Thesis (Master's degree in Legal Dentistry and Deontology) - State University of Campinas. Piracicaba, p. 31.

To preserve the dental element, some professionals do not remove the pulp for the preparation of the prosthesis, which can cause later pulpitis, with the consequent need for endodontic treatment, after removing the prosthesis on it. However, only the extreme followers of pulp conservation still insist on avoiding endodontic treatment.[86]

In the case of the loss of the prosthesis, the professional will have to bear the costs of a new prosthesis, having the right to charge for endodontic treatment.

Another hypothesis is that the professional has done the endodontic treatment and placed the prosthesis, and then the patient comes back with symptoms of infection. There may be two interpretations: either the treatment was incorrect, or the latent infection increased due to the new effort caused by the use of the prosthesis on the dental element.[87]

At the first possibility, the pain appears almost immediately and indicates the need to resume treatment of the canals. Trauma can also cause this sensitivity to the tooth's root due to a very high prosthesis. The professional can be held responsible if he ceases to act.

In the second possibility, the appearance of pain does not compromise the professional, as long as the infection is difficult to diagnose. Still, if you do not make a correct diagnosis and treatment, you will be held responsible.

Concerning fixed bridges, the dentist should be aware of the clinical details and the preparation of the material. In the clinical part, you should observe: the indication or not for the practice of the same, the preparation, and placement. The general rule is that for each support or foundation of the fixed bridge, only two elements are placed unsupported. Certain freedom is appropriate to the professional in this analysis and their accountability in the event of failure. It is generally not indicated to apply unsupported passing bridges from the incisors to the molars.[88]

---

[86]Lutz, Adolpho Gualter. **Mistakes and accidents in dentistry**. Ed. Est. From Graph Arts. Junior C.Mendes. Rio de Janeiro, 1938, p. 178.
[87]Lutz, Adolpho Gualter. **Mistakes and accidents in dentistry**. Ed. Est. From Arts Graph.. Junior C.Mendes. Rio de Janeiro, p.179,1938 .
[88] *Ibid.,* pp. 183-184

It should be taking care of the state of the roots that serve as a foundation, such as the need for endodontic treatment and if they are shaken, which would be the reason for the contraindication of the manufacture of the fixed prosthesis.

Shortly after the placement of a bridge, one of its elements falls; it is not proof of malpractice, only to repair the defect. Several can be the causes. First, if the roots on which it rests are shaken or destroyed.[89]

Secondly, one should analyze the quality of the dental cement used, whether enough material has been placed or the presence of air bubbles, and finally, the imperfections of the bridge itself.

The bridge should be perfectly adaptable or may fall by infiltration of oral substances or food residues or if it entered forced. The placement of a bridge that does not adapt perfectly, effortlessly, and without play to the dental elements of the arch constitutes malpractice.

When a bridge or unit prosthesis (crowns) falls, if there are no lesions of tissues of the mouth or fraud, the repair or replacement of the same and the replacement seems sufficient to us.

It may be that the patient invokes the damage suffered by the lack of the prosthesis, especially when it is apparent. However, the damage to chewing is challenging to demonstrate and will generally be of low value.[90]

The types of metals used in fixed and removable prostheses must be specified. In case of breakage due to poor quality of the material, it should be analyzed whether it was the material chosen by the patient and whether the guidelines and options of choice were given.

The patient should be aware that his dental elements will have to be worn often to place the prostheses on them when making fixed prostheses.

---

[89] Lutz, Adolpho Gualter. **Mistakes and accidents in dentistry**. Ed. Est. From Arts Graph.. Junior C.Mendes. Rio de Janeiro, p. 185, 1938.
[90] *Ibid.*, p. 186.

As for removable total dentures or dentures, one cannot have roots by extracting them under the prosthesis. In addition, patients should be aware of the probability of them not being firm in the upper or lower arches due to bone resorption, gingival tissue sagging, tuberosities, and other bone deformations.

The implants were invented precisely by the dissatisfaction of patients with total prostheses. A total prosthesis cannot be expected to meet all the expected requirements when the patient has his natural teeth. Many people hope the prosthesis gives them back what time has taken, such as a perfect smile and a younger appearance.

The fact is that the lack of retention of total prostheses alone does not demonstrate the dentist's malpractice but should be taken into account in all existing oral anatomy. The professional cannot promise their retention if it is clear that this cannot be achieved with the state of bone resorption when present.

Denture placement usually brings disappointment to the patient. When it is placed right after the extractions, they still have the disadvantage that, with alveolar resorption, the adaptation is no longer uniform. Annoyance is often also of psychic order and not only material.

4.4 Endodontics

Endodontic treatment occurs when tooth involvement has reached the extreme. The destruction of dental tissue even compromises the nerve inside or was affected due to trauma, a blow, for example.

Many are the causes of pulp disorders. They can be affected by trauma, abrasion, calcardium deposits within the pulp chamber, fillings acting on them, orthodontic corrections, chemicals and microbial metabolism, thermal, electrical, parasitic agents. They may also come from perishing or be a consequence of widespread disease.

Sometimes it is not easy to find out which tooth the pain originates from. It should be identified through sensitivity tests, such as thermal and radiological tests, so as not to treat pulpitis as if it were deep caries.

By saying that the canal was made, it is said that the nerve was removed from inside the tooth or done cleaning the nerve debris that deteriorated.

After removing all the material, disinfect and wait for the effect of the remedy placed inside is that the channel will be filled with the shutter material. Treatment should be done with absolute isolation and aseptically, avoiding contamination of the canal.

Usually, the channel is filled with gutta-percha. The inside of the canal can not be empty, but it would be a perfect place for the proliferation of bacteria, causing the formation of infection and abscesses.

Ingle[91] determined, through a work to evaluate endodontic treatments, what percentage of success of these treatments. Relating the causes of failures of endodontic treatments, it showed that 58% of them are due to incomplete filling of root canals.

Endodontics deals with the limit of success. Endodontic treatments have a 99% prospect of success, but others up to 40%, even in the hands of specialist professionals (verbal information).[92]

The success of the treatment depends a lot on the collaboration of the patient as well, both taking the medications at the time and in the psychological aspect, because the endodontic treatment, when presented, is involved a lot of pain, and the patient is already emotionally weakened.

---

[91] INGLE, John I. In: FRANCE, Beatriz Helena Sottile. **Civil and Criminal Liability of the Dentist,** 1993. Thesis (Master's degree in Legal Dentistry and Deontology) - State University of Campinas, Piracicaba, p. 18.
[92] Data obtained in the Endodontics Improvement Course at the Association of Dentists of Campinas in the second half of 2002.

In some cases, one cannot save the dental structures significantly damaged. Still, not so one can think of compensation, because the damaged tooth would be like a patient in an Intensive Care Unit (ICU), where the doctor tries to save it. Still, even if it does not, it is worth trying, and if even using all the technique correctly is not possible, one cannot blame the professional who did everything to save the dental element.

Cohen & Schwartz[93] conducted research involving the specialty of endodontics, and *according to the newspaper, The Dentist's Company of California* discussed, the most common causes of errors are: misdiagnosis or diagnostic failures; lack of use of the rubber dam; broken instruments; root perforations; lack of information for care; lack of postoperative instructions; lack of emergency care.

Severe infections may also occur during the irrigation of the canals and aspirations of instruments by the patient if the rubber dam is not present.

Silva and Calvielli,[94] according to studies conducted, dentistry researchers did not bother to present scientific research aimed at demonstrating, for legal purposes, the unpredictability of biological responses to specific treatments, including endodontic therapies.

The authors discuss what would be success and failure in endodontics from the expert's view, exposing that the affirmation of success or failure often does not have the legal connotation that could be given to him.

Paiva and Antoniazzi[95] observed that although radiographs evaluate the result of endodontic therapy, this criterion is not universal because radiographic images are only suggestive. Therefore, the radiographic standard should be in addition to the clinical bar.

---

[93]COHEN, S.; SCHWARTZ, *In*: FRANCE, Beatriz Helena Sottile. **Civil and Criminal Liability of the Dentist,** 1993. Thesis (Master's degree in Legal Dentistry and Deontology) - State University of Campinas, Piracicaba, p.34.

[94]SILVA, Moacyr da; CALVIELLI, Ida, T.P. Ethical and legal aspects of dentistry. *In*: FRANCE, Beatriz Helena Sottile. **Civil and Criminal Liability of the Dentist,** 1993. Thesis (Master's degree in Legal Dentistry and Deontology) - Estadual University of Campinas, Piracicaba, p. 40.

[95]PAIVA, J.G.; Antoniazzi, J.H. **Endodontics: Bases for clinical practice.** São Paulo: Artes Médicas. cap. 28, p. 24,1988.

Weine, cited by Paiva and Antoniazzi, recalls that the inadequate restoration is a much more significant failure factor than that conventional endodontic therapy, showing that dental elements can be lost even when correct the endodontic treatment.

It acts with fault the dentist, also when the preparation of a canal causes root trepanation, both by the lack of technique and by the wrong radiographic interpretation. Also, when breaking the reading instrument inside the root duct, for overuse or other reason.

Failure to observe isolation may also cause aspiration of endodontic files by the patient. The instrument can go to the airways during inspiration or end up in the stomach. In these cases, the professional will be responsible for the damages.

4.5 Aesthetic and dental restorative treatment

Dentistry is the specialization of dentistry that takes care of the most frequent treatment in dental offices, that is, restorations, known as "fillings."

Cavities are one of the most common lesions, and the lack of its diagnosis is one of the grossest errors. In cases of extensive cavities, it may be necessary to make a crown rather than restoration. However, if the professional indicates the preparation and the patient resolves to do the restoration, he cannot be held responsible in the event of a fall.

Dental science has evolved a lot, and many materials have been discovered to recover the damaged tooth in the most efficient, functional, and aesthetically speaking way.

The old silver amalgam restorations had mercury in their composition, which could cause contamination in the patient's body, as mercury accumulates in the body and is not eliminated. As a result, mercury allergy cases may lead to death. Currently, materials based on resins with tooth-like coloration and good strength are used.

Dentists are sought to change the old restorations and leave with an almost original smile, where it is so aesthetic that the presence of restorations is hardly noticed. It is possible to make characterizations in patients smokers, where the color is darker and presents certain spots.

The dentist may be charged for his failure to fail to imitate natural aesthetics. Often, the patient returns to the office, and the professional redo the service.

The aesthetic damage can be evaluated in dentistry through expertise, taking into account the aesthetic, phonetic, and masticatory aspects of the impaired dental element, as can be synthesized by the table offered by Genival Veloso de France,[96] since it synthesizes, in an obvious way, the formative aspects of aesthetic/moral damage:

Aesthetic, phonetic, and masticatory value of teeth[97]

Dental piece	AESTHETIC value	Phonetic Value	Masticatory value
Central incisor	100	100	40
Lateral incisor	90	90	40
Canine	80	80	70
1st premolar	70	50	60

---

[96] FRANCE, G.V.de. **Medicine Legal.** 6th ed. Ed. Guanabara Koogan, Rio de Janeiro, p. 141, 2001.
[97] ARBENZ, G.O. *apud* FRANCE, G.V.de. **Medicine Legal.** 6th ed. Ed. Guanabara Koogan, Rio de Janeiro, p. 141, 2001.

2nd premolar	60	40	70
1st molar	50	--	100
2nd molar	40	--	90
3rd molar	--	--	--

This table shows that the third molar does not have much aesthetic, phonetic, or masticatory value, but it would have a high prosthetic value if a prosthesis can be performed to replace the missing teeth.

Thus, Álvaro Dória,[98] for the 100% of the aesthetic function, proposes the following values for a Hemi-arch (representing only 25% of the entire dental arch):

Dental part	Aesthetic percentage
Central incisor	6 %
Lateral incisor	6 %
Canine	6 %

---

[98]DÓRIA, Álvaro *In* ARBENZ, G.O. *apud* FRANCE, G.V.de. **Medicine Legal.** 6th ed. Ed. Guanabara Koogan, Rio de Janeiro, p. 141, 2001.

1st premolar	5 %
2nd premolar	2 %
1st molar	0 %
2nd molar	0 %
3rd molar	0 %

Hentze, for the 100% integrity [99] of the masticatory function of each tooth, establishes the following percentages for a Hemi-arc (representing only 25% of the total of the arch dentária, the whole being 25 % X 4 = 100 %):

Dental part	% functional masticatory
Incisivo central	1 %
Incisivo lateral	1 %
Canino	2 %
1sr premolar	3 %
2nd premolar	3 %
1st molar	5 %
2nd molar	5 %
3rd molar	5 %

As for phonetic function, a percentage loss is evaluated in each dental part in the following indexes for a Hemi-arch (representing only 25% of the total dental arch):

---

[99] HENTZE In ARBENZ apud FRANCE, G.V.de. **Medicine Legal.** 6th ed. Ed. Guanabara Koogan, Rio de Janeiro, p. 141, 2001.

Dental part	Perda fonética
Central incisor	8 %
Lateral incisor	8 %
Canino	6 %
1st premolar	2 %
2nd premolar	1 %
1st molar	0 %
2nd molar	0 %
3rd molar	0 %

In addition to the aspects treated, one can also consider the decrease in tooth function in chewing by the non-occlusion with the antagonist's tooth, called the coefficient of antagonism, reaching 50% of the missing tooth.

In practice, what happens is that experts, when responding to the requirements of tooth weakness and the functional loss, are more concerned with masticatory indexes.

The principle that only the anterior teeth are that they have more value is not accurate today due to the various existing rehabilitation techniques. Even the third molar, as we said, now has its value because they are essential for the manufacture of prostheses, functioning as pillars.

Deciduous or "milk" teeth should be restored and preserved, functioning as a guide for permanent tooth eruption, and its premature loss may lead to the closure of the space required for the permanent tooth to erupt.

Thus, we conclude that the mere lack of occlusal contact of the teeth can compromise the health of the teeth, leading to their loss in the future, reiterating that dentistry is a profession of details, and the inattentive professional, can be held responsible.

4.6 Maxillo-facial surgery

The buccomaxillofacial specialty is very close to Medicine. Therefore, the surgeon has to have in-depth knowledge of various subjects contained in the doctor's training.

It acts in emergencies rooms and ICUs, serving the victims of polytraumatized accidents regarding facial and oral structures.

Many fractures of the jaw and jaw occur, requiring containment with metal pins and moorings with stainless steel wires to reduce the fracture, and the patient will have to stay in this situation for months until the solidification of the bone happens, feeding almost always through a straw.

It also acts in restorative surgeries when it is necessary to reposition the maxilla or jaw that is very protruding or retruded, working together with the orthodontist determining the new position in which the jaws should be placed.

The legal foundations for this action are in the Code of Dental Ethics, chapter IX, "Hospital Dentistry," inserted in resolution CFO - 179/91 of 19-12-91, which states:

> Article 16: it is the responsibility of the dentist to hospitalize and assist patients in public and private hospitals, with and without philanthropic character, respecting the technical-administrative standards of the institutions.

> Article 17: dental activities performed in the hospital will comply with the rules of the Federal Council.
>
> Article 18: it constitutes an ethical infraction, even in a hospital environment, to perform surgical intervention outside the scope of dentistry

Article 41 of Resolution No. 185 of April 26, 1996, of the Federal Council of Dentistry, defines the specialty:

> Art. 41. Oral-Maxillofacial Surgery and Traumatology is the specialty that aims at the diagnosis and surgical and adjuvant treatment of diseases, traumas, lesions, and congenital anomalies acquired from the masticatory apparatus and attachments and associated craniofacial structures.

There is a doubt about the field of action of specialists and physicians because there is a medical specialty entitled Craniofacial Surgery and the plastic surgeons who began to invade the area of oral-maxillofacial surgery.

Resolution 185/93, which is found in Annex C, contains the articles that establish the participation of physicians working together with the oral-maxillofacial specialist and in the arts. 43 to 49, set the limits of action and fields of cooperation between these professionals.

As I mentioned earlier, the oral-maxillofacial surgeon has a mean obligation because he undertakes to use all his expertise and technique to try to save the patient's facial structures, but not being obliged with the result.

Just as plastic surgeries are not obligations of result, as is known to the medical-scientific class, if the techniques are not used correctly and some problem occurs, the professional can also be held responsible for aesthetic and moral damage.

Studies show that the skin can react in various ways, depending on each individual, often getting more or less thick and reddish scars, leaving an unaesthetic aspect in the healing phase (verbal information).[100]

The surgeon can be held responsible for aesthetic damage if he acts with recklessness, negligence, and malpractice when caring for the patient and will answer for the damage caused if his mistake is proven.

---

[100] KFOURI NETO, Miguel. In : **SYMPOSIUM ON THE CIVIL AND CRIMINAL LIABILITY OF THE DOCTOR.** Campinas, São Paulo: 2002.

In case of unnecessary extractions of teeth, even with the patient's consent and in writing, the dentist will be committing serious misconduct from a legal and moral point of view.[101]

It acts with guilt also when it causes fracture and mandibular dislocation when extracting a retained or impacted tooth. Attention should be paid after surgery, observing the appearance of abscesses and other degenerative diseases.

Although not very time-consuming, dental extractions are an irreversible act and lack the patient's consent and an indication that justifies such a procedure.[102]

The extraction of a tooth without the patient's consent may characterize a criminal and civil body injury. Also, exclude the possibility of extraction of a tooth, and the abstention of the professional can cause the increase and spread of infection, later requiring a surgical intervention of more significant proportions.[103]

It is best to obtain written consent and have radiographic examinations before the procedure, avoiding extractions of wrong teeth and diagnostic errors. For example, there are cases of molars with cement welding the roots of one with the neighbors, and when extracting, it occurs of leaving two teeth instead of one.[104]

Due to pain, some patients prefer the extraction to be subjected to a conservative treatment, such as endodontic treatment, which in cases of pulpitis, requires several treatment sessions and monetary expenses, and often, with the unsafe result. The dentist who attends the patient's will, in these cases, would not justify a criminal or civil procedure.[105]

Extractions are contraindicated in hemophiliac patients due to probability of a hemorrhage. Profuse hemorrhages also occur due to the inferior dental artery rupture and the extraction of a tooth bound to an angioma.[106]

---

[101]**Dental Ethic Code**, art. 3, I . CFO Resolution 179/91 of 19/1/91. **Federal Council of Dentistry**, Rio de Janeiro.

[102]Lutz, Adolpho Gualter. **Mistakes and accidents in dentistry**. Ed. Est. From Graph Arts. Junior C.Mendes. Rio de Janeiro, p.82, 1938.
[103] *Ibid.*, p.85.
[104] *Ibid.*, p.88.
[105] *Ibid.*, p.91.

A tooth that escapes from the forceps or a lever directed toward the pharynx can cause swallowing of the extracted tooth, which can cause closure of the troat or even go to the lungs.[107]

Excessive force can cause alveolar trauma, and if it slips, it may injure the tongue, cheeks, palate, or floor of the mouth. Fractures of the mandible or maxillary occur, requiring posterior surgical restraint, which requires several months of treatment. [108]

Extraction can cause nerve damage such as the lower alveolar, located near the lower third molar, and may cause facial paralysis after the procedure.

A dental infection can progress to phlegm and to osteomyelitis, which by invading bone tissue, can cause its mortification and may originate from an incomplete extraction, when a tooth extraction is done included in the region of existing osteomyelitis or when the cavity resulting from an extraction becomes infected and propagates the infection to more significant bone extensions, which demonstrates the great responsibility of the professional when performing an apparently easy extraction.[109]

The dentist should not allow himself to be coerced to extract a tooth, guided by the patient's indication as his pain may originate from other infectious processes that cause that sensitivity, and when removing the tooth, he will be surprised that the pain continues.

4.7 Periodontics

This specialty has been widespread in most countries. Although unnecessary dental extractions are not made, due only to the presence of caries and use of all available resources to save teeth, there is a problem of periodontal diseases.

---

[106] *Ibid.*, p. 101.
[107] *Ibid.*, p. 104.
[108] Lutz, Adolpho Gualter. **Mistakes and accidents in dentistry**. Ed. Est. From Graph Arts. Junior C.Mendes. Rio de Janeiro, p.110, 1938.
[109] *Ibid.*, p.131.

These diseases are linked to various factors such as stress, poor tooth brushing, advanced age, and other factors. Like every dental specialty, periodontics has its techniques and scientific norms in combating injuries located in the periodontium, in the space at the limit between the tooth and the gums.

In surgeries to repair gingival tissue that has undergone resorption, for example, there is a whole technique and care for cutting the flap that will be used to cover the dental element.

In treating infections, one must have the knowledge and mastery of medications to achieve their cure and clean tartars and other organic materials deposited in the periodontium.

Sometimes the patient presents all the tooth elements softened due to periodontic disease, and the professional should use all his knowledge to try to restore oral health. Still, it is also not a result obligation.

Suppose the professional uses every technique correctly and does everything possible, within the norms of periodontics, not assuming an obligation of result. In that case, he is excluded from being held responsible for aesthetic damage.

It acts with guilt when it does not correctly remove the stones and does not clarify to the patient the importance of their participation for the future control of plaque, which is essential for preventing dental structure.

The professional should alert the patient about excessive tooth mobility and indicate treatment in the office itself or indicate to a specialist.

Periodontics has worked together with the specialty of implants in healing implants, worrying about hygiene and preventing the formation of infections around the implant.

4.8 Dental radiology

There are many radiological clinics specializing in dentistry today. They have devices for panoramic radiography, to have a view of all teeth in single radiography; teleradiography used to analyze the angles and positioning of the teeth about craniometric points, used in orthodontics and also perform, among others, periapical radiography of a tooth or group of adjacent teeth, the most common being.

All these types aim to facilitate and assist the dentist in diagnosing and planning the treatment, identifying, for example, the presence of cavities, the need to do an endodontic treatment or not, the existence of infections, fractures, etc. It is vital in endodontic treatment, where several radiographs are made, usually in offices, where it is necessary to have an X-ray device.

Tambura[110] made a radiographic analysis of root conduit fillings classifying them as success or failure. The author concludes that many endodontic failures have been technical failures that radiography presented as a diagnostic information method.

According to their technical standards, the dental radiology professional, using sophisticated equipment and radiographic development techniques, should support a diagnosis for correct treatment.

Radiographs are often twisted, or diagnoses are wrong, causing dental professionals to make mistakes.

In these cases, proving the negligence, malpractice, or recklessness of dental radiology professionals, they will be subject to a civil damage process due to the aesthetic damage that other professionals cause to their patients, being through direct action or by way of return of the other impaired professional.

---

[110]TAMBURUS, J.R. **Radiographic research of the successes and successes of endodontic treatment**. In: Magazine of the . São Paulo Association of Dentists. V. 37, n.1, Jan/Feb. 1983.

Several dental insurance scans require the initial and final radiographs of each procedure, including restorations, requiring excessive use of radiographs in the office, even for simple procedures such as restorations.

Therefore, it is necessary to use a plumbiferous apron for the patient and the professional exposed to radiation daily, preferably having a screen with lead protection.

Acts with guilt when it employs improper technique or does not take care of the excellent quality of radiographic revelation, inducing a false diagnosis.

4.9 Oral pathology /semiology

When starting treatment for anamnesis, the patient is asked several questions about their general health. For example, if you have had diseases such as hepatitis, if you are a cardioid, you have high blood pressure, etc. Then you have a clinical examination of the oral cavity, where, among other things, the oral tissues, if some repetitive movement causes injuries or traumas, are analyzed.

The pathology studies diseases that can act on the oral mucosa and bone structures and are numerous, such as herpes, malignant and benign tumors, and diseases of the salivary glands.

Semiology, complementing the study of diseases, is concerned with their symptoms and signs. For example, stains on the mouth, abnormal growth of tissues, and fissures; must all be checked.

The general practitioner should identify reddish or purplish spots on the patient's oral mucosa in the anamnesis in his office and identify them as possible diseases.

Caution should be taken, observing if it has any traumatic origin, such as the use of prostheses, continuous use of cigarettes, drinking scorching drinks frequently, such as chimarrão in southern Brazil, among other causes that cause a constant trauma.

The professional also must refer these patients to a specialist, as it is the general practitioners who have the opportunity first to observe these lesions in their patients and should prevent them from the importance of a more accurate examination, such as biopsy.

The professional can also be held responsible for aesthetic damage if negligence does not observe the injury and if it grows, causing more significant damage to the patient.

Acts with guilt when you set the wrong diagnosis in identifying an injury.

4.10 Pediatric dentistry

It is dentistry focused on the dental treatment of children, working with preventing caries through education about correct brushing, using sealants on teeth, and using space-maintaining devices, among others.

In the old days, many "milk" teeth were extracted because since another tooth would be born, there was no need to treat the tooth that would be changed.

Today it is known the importance of preserving deciduous teeth, keeping the space for permanent tooth eruption, and serving as a guide.

A previous preparation is done through preparatory consultations for the children to become familiar with the office and treatments.

Endodontics and prosthesis techniques can recover compromised teeth, and if not oriented in this sense, the dentist can be held responsible in case of unnecessary extraction.

Deciduous or milk teeth should be kept in the dental arch until the correct age so that it serves as a guideline for the eruption of the permanent tooth.

It acts with guilt that condemns a temporary dental element rather than re-refounding it, as it would serve as a guide for the positioning of the permanent successor; in the extraction of destroyed temporary teeth, but with a chance of recovery through the prosthesis, causing subsequent occlusion disorder in the permanent dentition of the child, etc.

These examples can be questioned as aesthetic damage, negligence, recklessness, or malpractice of the dentist, extracting a tooth unnecessarily without trying to save it, or not indicating the patient to a specialist. It only fits aesthetic damage if the professional did not act in compliance with all the norms and techniques of the profession and if he did not assume an obligation of result.

As examples of errors in pediatric dentistry, we can also mention the stains on the teeth due to excessive application of fluoride, various aesthetic damages, such as speech obstruction, the need for the use of corrective devices and their non-indication, fluoride intake due to the lack of the use of the sucker and the tray, restorations with the vertical dimension very high, hindering occlusion and may compromise the permanent tooth in formation, etc.

The ingestion of fluoride at the time of application without trays or sucking can lead to death because it is a toxic substance.

4.11 Dental anesthesia

Brazilian dentists are qualified for topical anesthesia, local or regional anesthesia, in addition to anesthetics and ointments, spray anesthetics, and gargle.

When the patient arrives at the doctor's office as an adult, he has usually had anesthesia several times. However, it is still necessary to make an anamnesis, a questionnaire, asking for several details of the person's health.

Ask if you are allergic to any medication, have a heart problem, chronic disease, condition, bleeding, etc. In the case of a woman, whether you are pregnant, breastfeeding, etc.

In addition to all these details, one should take into account the psychological part of the patient: if he suffers fainting if he becomes very nervous because anesthesia will last less time, which has, as a consequence, an anesthetic effect of shorter time, and application of a more significant amount of anesthetic.

All these details should be observed, including the professional must have a resuscitation device, that is, an oxygen device, in case of fainting. In addition, the patient must sign the questionnaire to the final, proving the prudence of the professional.

According to the manufacturer, there is also a limit of anesthetic tubes that can be applied, which is stipulated in the package leaflet of the product.

If these steps are not taken, and a problem occurs, the professional may also be held responsible for aesthetic and moral damage.

The legal aspects of anesthesia and its effects are dealt with by Law 1,314 of January 17, 1951, giving the dentist the right to establish treatment and art. 129, § 1, item II of the Penal Code, which deals with bodily injury of a serious nature, causing life-threatening, including in this article, anaphylactic shock due to the application of anesthesia.

It will hardly occur with local anesthesia, commonly applied in the dental office, being more likely in surgeries in hospitals, where general anesthesia of the patient is necessary.

As a consequence of anesthesia through injection, diseases such as infection, lesions at the injection site, needle rupture, and lesions are attributed to the toxic effect of the injected substances.

In the case of infections, one should have good asepsis of the site to avoid them. Needles and tubes are disposable and should not be reused. In case of liquid left inside the pipes, it should not be reused, as it can ser a vehicle for transmitting diseases and infection from one patient to another.

Anesthesia should also not be applied to infected tissues, which may cause the spread of the infection into the bloodstream and neighboring tissues of the site. If possible, trounce, or regional application is made, or else, the patient will be medicated, and only after the infection kickback will act on the site.

There are accidents due to errors in the technique of application of injections. A possible consequence is the formation of a hematoma due to the disruption of small vessels, including those that irrigate the muscles. In addition, it may cause trismus at the time of truncate anesthesia. [111]

In addition to bleeding, with conseqüente pain and tumefaction, ulcers may arise, due to necrosis of the injected tissue, occurring more in the fibro-mucosa palatine, being painful and difficult to heal.[112]

The needle may break in the mouth's tissues, and if it is not possible to remove it, surgery will be required. However, this type of accident is rare due to disposable needles.

Symptoms such as transient pallor, malaise, shorthand, and syncope are common after anesthesia and may even be fainting. However, death in the dentist's chair is rare and would be more linked to the patient's heart problems, which should be investigated at the time of the anamnesis made before any procedure.[113]

Podem needles cause nerve damage, especially in lower third molars or wisdom teeth. Anesthesia in the floor of the mouth can reach the lingual nerve, which can cause severe pain, the tumefaction of the corresponding edge of the tongue, or even trismus and necrosis of soft tissues.[114]

---

[111]Lutz, Adolpho Gualter. **Mistakes and accidents in dentistry**. Ed. Est. From Graph Arts. Junior C.Mendes. Rio de Janeiro, 1938, p. 65.
[112] *Ibid.*, p. 67.
[113] *Ibid.*, p.73.
[114] *Ibid.*, p. 80.

Regional hemi-mandible anesthesia may compromise the facial nerve, resulting in paresthesias and transient or long-term paralysis.[115]

4.12 Dentistry

Social dentistry deals with the oral health of the population. For example, it makes assessments in schools to know the index of teeth affected in children, statistically analyzing decayed, lost, or filling teeth.

Children have a higher incidence of the number of caries. In this prevention work, professionals work together with the municipalities to fluoridate the drinking water, which is an excellent way of preventing caries.

If the professional errs in the amount of fluoride concentration, it can cause fluorosis, with consequent grayish spots on the teeth, intoxications, and even lead death.

4.13 Stomatology

This specialty deals with diseases of the mouth and attached structures, including oral manifestations of systemic diseases that may interfere with treatment.

It deals with prevention, diagnosis, and prognosis, with a means obligation about prevention and diagnosis, and may result in the performance of complementary tests.

5 THE INSURANCE FOR MORAL AND MATERIAL DAMAGE

---

[115] *Ibid.*, p. 81.

The problem of lawsuits against dentists has spread in such a way that, through the initiative of the Association of Dentists of the State of São Paulo, is currently being offered professionals liability insurance, together with the monthly contribution slip so that the professional will not lose what he earned during years of work, in a single dental error, which is often even statistically proven, which frequently occurs, such as the case of failures in endodontic treatments, commonly called canal treatment.

This insurance is already a routine practice in other countries, such as the United States. Conrad et al. report that more than 95% of dentists in the United States of America have professional liability insurance.[116]

Insurance is based on the same principles as other insurance. The contribution of many individuals to cover any indemnities resulting from the error of any of the taxpayers, as a way to minimize the effects of compensation, is expected to occur sporadically so as not to extinguish the fund.

We believe that the error is present in the most diverse professional areas and that in the history of every individual, hardly anyone can analyze his conscience, say that he has never made a mistake and that, indeed, some work could have gotten better.

This search for perfection is inherent to human nature, and man is constantly evolving, looking for new techniques that ensure a higher rate of success in treatments.

Even revolutionary accessories such as electron microscopy for endodontic treatments, such as orthodontic techniques with minimized forces, are subject to failure.

---

[116]CONRAD, D.A. et al. Malpractice premius in 1992: Results of a National Survey of Dentists J. Am. Dent. Assoc. 126(7): 1045-1056, Jul. 1995. *In*: FRANCE, B.H. S. *1998*. Thesis (PhD in Legal Dentistry and Deontology). **The Professional Civil Liability Insurance of the Dentist**, p.95.

And it is through the analysis of these techniques and procedures employed, that the professional will be analyzed in the case of a judicial process.

This insurance aims not to allow the dentist, to be threatened in his day to day, to have to pay compensation, where despite having acted rigorously in the technique employed, even so, he is condemned for failure or error.

The reality of Brazil today is that many general practitioners charge about 30 reais to do a dental extraction, and many popular prices have been practiced so that the population can have access to dental treatment.

Our country is reputed to be a country of toothless, despite a large number of dentists, even being higher than recommended by the World Health Organization (WHO).

Now, this does not prevent very high indemnities from being stipulated, being of practice indemnities in the amount of 20 thousand reais, the amount that requires a lot of work time to be earned, in a dental office that tends to the middle class down.

So, these lawsuits alert the professional, who has to protect himself. You must have all the documentation, files, and a desk to help with the bureaucratic part, in addition to equipment and appliances, such as X-rays, apart from the cost of liability insurance, further making dental treatment more expensive.

But the professional, even taking these precautions, has to be warned because these insurances do not cover all indemnities and have their limits.

They expressly exclude coverage for aesthetic damage, experimental techniques or unauthorized medications, prohibited interventions, damages resulting from breach of professional secrecy, and radiation and chemotherapy treatments.

Many professionals act as employees of service companies, and these companies do not have insurance. Therefore, there is no way for the professional to charge the patients too much to take out the insurance. An equation capable of making insurance compulsory would be found to make insurance economically viable.

We understand that it will become mandatory here in Brazil, too, from the moment the laws make concrete for insurance companies, which would be included in the expression "moral damage" and to what extent the patient can avail himself of the Consumer Protection Code, or it would be a considerable amount of lawsuits and indemnifications that no company could bear. Perhaps that is why, to this day, civil liability insurance has not been widespread.

We emphasize that authors such as Genival Veloso França and Miguel Kfouri Neto show some advantages of professional liability insurance, such as :[117][118]

> - A better way of settlement of damages;
> - Improve the condition of freedom and safety at work;
> - Ensuring social balance and public order;
> - A better form of social justice;
> - The best form of social security itself;
> - Free doctor and patient from painful and time-consuming processes;
> - Avoid exploitation, ruin, injustice, and iniquities;
> - It is independent of the economic situation of the cause of the damage;
> - Correct the victim's property demeanor;
> - Contribute to the surplus of the system in programs to prevent damage;
> - Stimulate social solidarity;
> - It has flaws but has the most significant number of benefits and advantages;
> - Corrects the fact that the patient is totally forgotten and the doctor falsely remembered.

The adoption of insurance does not solve the problem. It just minimizes its consequences. It is impossible to adopt The American standards here because they are different realities.

Miguel Kfouri himself, in[119] his work, comments:

> Thus, the system balances in a fragile way: the injured still seek little to repair the damage caused to them by medical professionals; the physicians, when demanded, try to defend themselves, attributing to fatality the harmful event; hospitals, in turn, do not always have the resources to satisfy the indemnifications or, about the doctors who are part of their clinical staff, emphasize that the responsibility is always personal of the doctor, that there is no bond and other claims by the professional.

Professor Gustavo Tepedino says that it is not in the Brazilian tradition to contract civil liability insurance by the doctor or hospitals, perhaps because the amounts of compensation imposed by the judiciary do not yet pose a threat to professional activity, which can also be

---

[117] FRANCE, Genival Veloso de. **Medical Law**. 6. Ed. São Paulo : BYK-Procienx Editorial Fund, 1994.
[118] KFOURI NETO, Miguel. **Medical Liability**. São Paulo: Ed. Revista dos Tribunais: 4th ed., p. 27 1999.
[119] *Ibid.*,p.25.

applied to the dentistry professional[120].

There are several types of policies, covering the acts of auxiliaries and other employees of the office or only the acts of the dentist. It is always better to have more comprehensive coverage. Insurance pays a certain amount per policy, even if there is more than one occurrence in the same period.

I understand that the most significant disadvantages of this insurance are: due to the dissemination of the use of malpractice insurance, there may be an increase in the incidence of litigation and convictions to dentists because who will pay the compensation is the insurer.

Insurance does not cover the ethical and criminal consequences that the professional may suffer. Not even those that the publicity of your mistake can bring to your clientele, which weighs heavily in a profession where it is crucial to indicate one customer to another.

The Federal Constitution authorizes the accumulation of indemnification for material and moral damages arising from the same fact. These convictions are even more significant than the compensation for criminal damage.

But nowadays, insurance of civil liability begins to emerge with coverage for moral damage, such as the professionals of the Associations of Dentists of the State of São Paulo, who pay on time the monthly fees, are entitled to insurance of one hundred thousand reais, being fifty thousand, the ceiling for compensation for moral damage.

As mentioned earlier, the form of insurance financing would also have the side effect of raising the cost of dental services since it would have to be passed on to the final consumer, the patient, and the user of health services, which as a rule, are already expensive or inadequate.

The professional with several jobs are more prone to error due to a work overload due to the natural loss of reflexes and body wear. However, having insurance, he is convinced that he is not at risk or that these are minimal.

---

[120] TEPEDINO, Gustavo. Civil Law issues. Rio de Janeiro, Editora Renovar, 2nd edition, 2001.

It can be said that insurance would create an indemnity industry in Brazil. Still, on the other hand, this would require constant recycling and updating of dental knowledge, as well as an improvement of service providers committed to the quality standard.

Brazilians don't have a tradition of hiring insurance, but this is changing. It is necessary to reward the good and make the bad professionals judged by their peers, taking them away from the function.

The professional is sought for his degree of specialization by indicating to other patients, and the patient never asks if the dentist has liability insurance. Therefore, the argument that insurance would be the good of bad professionals because of a natural selectivity in the very contracting of the product is an exaggeration.

Having an insurance policy is no guarantee that treatment is guaranteed. On the contrary, it could even demonstrate the possible insecurity of the dentist, who would be taking a defensive attitude.

It is desired to seek to eliminate the punishable dental error and not palliative to avoid the bankruptcy of dentists who will suffer a lawsuit. The punishable dental error resulting from omission, malpractice, negligence, or recklessness of human error, which stems from the person's fallible condition, is different.

The latter is unpredictable, and the first can and should be avoided, whether through courses of improvement or specialization, the use of better materials and equipment, such as in the endodontic treatment, the use of the apical locator device, or the use of a new orthodontic technique, with softer forces of tooth movement, professional awareness, etc.

6 RESEARCH DONE IN THE SPECIAL CIVIL COURT

In this research, data were collected regarding cases against dentists in the Special Civil Court of Campinas-São Paulo - Paulista University Annex (UNIP).

The cases were checked from the year 2000 until July 2003. This survey aims to see if the demand for compensation by consumers has increased over the years, considering that access to the Court is free, precisely so that they find their contents satisfied without having to bear expenses with the legal process.

Some primary data were collected each year, i.e.:

1. Number of cases per year;
2. Types of proceedings (repay, moral damage, etc.);
3. Dental specialties involved;
4. The average amount of indemnity;
5. Whether there was conciliation or a hearing of inquiry and trial was required.

Concerning the amounts, we remember that in civil court are accepted issues whose indemnities do not exceed the amount of 40 minimum wages.

In its first year of operation, in 2000, there were about 3487 processes, and referring to dental professionals and dental clinics were about six processes, which statistically gives a low percentage of 0.17 % of the total demands, which is something inexpressive because of the large number of dentists and the general population seeking their services.

Six cases were of moral damage, two were asking for treatment reconstitution in the case of orthodontic treatments, and one for collection.

Most of them were all settled in conciliation sessions, made with conciliators, and approved the agreements by the magistrates.

This shows that the legal issues that arrived at the small cases court and those that came were made agreements. In 2001, 5641 cases were admitted, referring to the dealt with dentists, about five processes.

Of this total, three referred again to the end of a contract in orthodontic treatments, a conviction in cash, an obligation to do, and another termination of a contract with cash return.

Of these five, three were against agreements with dental clinics, most of them being the specialty of orthodontics. Most were reconciled before the hearing of instruction and judgment, and the values turned around one thousand reais.

In 2002 there were about 7845 processes and about six processes related to dental treatments. Of this amount, two referred to the end of contracts pertaining to orthodontic treatments and three returns of amounts paid. Conciliatory agreements were made in three cases, and three others were for an instructional and trial hearing. The indemnities, when they occurred, did not exceed one thousand reais, even in cases where the ceiling of 40 minimum wages was requested.

A process dealt with the prosthesis specialty, where a lower removable prosthesis was made, but the patient could not use it for more than three months due to a periodontal problem she had in a lower canine. Having entered the process, it was resolved still in conciliation, having been returned about 200 reais but having to replace the prosthesis.

The exciting thing, in this case, is that the professional who made the prosthesis charged a value well below that would be about 400 reais in a general practitioner, according to the Dentistry Board of Campinas's reimbursement table, and can reach 1000 reais in a prosthesis specialist, where the price takes into account, mainly, the reputation of the professional.

The return of the prosthesis to the dentist does not compensate for the work at all because the prostheses are made individually. This prosthesis will be unusable and will not refund the expense of the professional. The return is, in addition to having the money back, the patient still does not enjoy it.

Often, the socio-economic reality of the Brazilian takes him to the dentist, already with the elements badly damaged. Among the treatments available as implants and fixed prostheses, ends up opting for the most into account, that is, the removable prosthesis, but many people do not adapt to them.

What would be the correct procedure, then? The professional should x-type all dental elements of the patient to see if they have any resorptions and bone compromises not visible to the naked eye. You should have the patient sign the indication of several better treatments that you did not accept for financial reasons and keep all the documentation.

The professional would be protected if the patient, aware of her bone resorption, chose to make the prosthesis and then could not use it. But the less favored population seeking treatment with a prosthesis, who have already lost several dental elements, often can not even do a complete radiographic examination, with panoramic radiographs that cost about 60 reais, or a third of the value of the prosthesis that paid.

We understand that the socio-economic factors of the population, the economic level of the patient who seeks to make the treatment more into account, even if it is not the most indicated, and the fact that the professional does not charge the price of a specialist, are taken into account for the determination of the professional's guilt.

In the year 2003 to July, there were about 2249 cases, seven against clinics and dental professionals.

After a metal and ceramic prosthesis was made, the patient began to have bleeding problems with breakage and softening. So, this process dealt with the specialty of a prosthesis. It was not possible to prior conciliation, having gone to hearing of instruction and judgment. The amount of indemnification turned around eight hundred reais.

In another process, from the specialty of orthodontics, a patient paid three installments for the manufacture of a mobile orthodontic appliance, which broke three times, and having been lost the patient's trust in the dental insurance professional, the patient decided to file the action to have his paid portions returned.

The conciliation hearing was left fruitless, an instructional and trial hearing was held, and the clinic had to return about 200 reais.

The third case was moral damage and was asked the limit of 40 minimum wages, which was around 8 thousand reais. It was about a dental agreement that included the customer's name improperly in the Credit Protection Office (SPC), even after the client had canceled the deal, ending the issuance of bank slips, which did not occur.

The conciliation remained fruitless, having gone to the trial instruction hearing, and the compensation ended in around one thousand reais.

There was a professional process against a dental equipment company for the delay in delivering the equipment in the office within the established deadline, causing loss of patients and rental scares, condominiums, etc., for maintenance of the commercial room. It was a charge action with moral damages.

Although this process has not yet been finalized, we find fascinating the aspect that also, the dental professional can have his work and efficiency compromised by the responsibility of third parties, such as the non-delivery of purchased equipment, the delivery of damaged materials, expired or altered consumables; medication purchased with altered effectiveness and all kinds of failure resulting from third parties, dental products factories or dental retailers.

There was a lawsuit for moral damages for improper collection by a dental agreement, with values around the ceiling of 8,000 reais, with conciliation hearing remaining fruitless. Before the hearing of instruction and trial, the parties agreed and extinguished the process.

The sixth process was to return the amount of a patient who began to pay for a canal treatment and was then discovered to be pregnant in the specialty of endodontics. He stopped paying the tuition and then asked for restitution of what he had paid, about 300 reais.

The conciliation hearing was left fruitful, and the return of 100 reais was agreed upon.

From the data obtained, some observations can be drawn regarding the current situation of the search for compensation against dentists in the Special Civil Court of Campinas - Unip Annex.

This work aimed to analyze the relationship of the dentist's activity to civil liability, including the implications of his acts in cases of treatment errors in the factual legal claims, in the universe of the Special Civil Court of Campinas - Annex UNIP.

We want to discuss the relationship of the professional dentist, acting as a service provider in front of the patient, who is a consumer according to the Consumer Protection Code, with its legal implications in the case of unsuccessful treatments.

The relationship of the professional with his patient, inspired mainly through trust, has become a consumer relationship. If the patient likes the product, fine, but if he doesn't, he will want to be compensated.

We try to show that there is a demand for damages in the court against dental professionals. We try to clarify, among other doubts, which have increased the actions against dentists and which specialties generate the most significant conflict and the average value of the causes.

We understand the increase in the number of cases against dentists. However, few in the Court were not only due to the existence of new laws that defend the patient but to an awareness of consumer rights, which is very widespread today.

The truth is that dental science treats a living organism. The human body has biological reactions that are not fully understood. Still, one can do a statistical survey, for example, as it already exists, to have an idea if the therapy of a channel can have 40, 60, 100%, or another percentage of chances of success.

The relationship between the work of the dental professional is not exact or, put, a relationship to the consumption of goods because the success of the treatment depends on numerous factors, such as the general health of the patient, whether it is cardiac, diabetic if it has high blood pressure, etc.

Patient cooperation also has a large share in achieving success or failure. Therefore, all instructions, prescriptions, absences of the patient in the consultations, and other details of the patient's clinical record should be documented and signed.

To be more enlightening, the simple lack of consultation in endodontic treatment can trigger an inflammatory process causing the failure of treatment. Still, at the time, the patient assumed so, will say only that he paid for a service and ended up losing his tooth.

For this small explanation, we see that the relationship of the professional/patient should be surrounded by documentation, very well explanatory and signed so that it has the effect of allowing the exemption of responsibility of the dentist.

The professional does not work alone but will answer for the error of each member of his office as a secretary, assistant, dental hygienist, etc.

Therefore, it is important to take care of all the details of the office, including biosafety, that is, the correct sterilization of instruments and the dental work environment, and be attentive to the legal implications of their non-compliance.

FINAL CONSIDERATIONS

The Constitution guarantees the right to health for all, providing public services and delegating to third parties part of the responsibility. Therefore, health professionals respond civilly, both in the public and private areas, to possible errors, as was commented on in this work regarding the dental error.

We believe that you have tended to adopt mandatory liability insurance in Brazil, as is done in the United States. Without it, the professional cannot practice the profession. Therefore, it is appropriate to create legislation that creates national insurance for the dental area to cover the damage caused by professionals and reduce their costs.

Currently, the professional can be held responsible for a problem in the care of the office, asepsis, or the lack of updating in the dental area. Whenever the patient feels injured, the professional should be well guarded with all documentation.

Dentists must be instructed by the legal provisions of the Civil Code, Penal Code, Consumer Law Code, and Code of Dental Ethics. It must have professional training, which in addition to the technique, is based on legal concepts because it can not claim in court ignorance of the law. If you work with the honesty of purpose and technical knowledge, not guaranteeing an obligation of result, it will hardly be held judiciously liable.

About the Consumer Protection Code, in article 14, § 4, where it says that the dentist will be held responsible by verifying his guilt, some authors understand that it will not always be their fault, as in the case of the dentist committing to perform an obligation of result and this is not reached.

In this case, they understand that the professional will objectively answer the damage caused to the patient. They also suggest the change of the article, adding to this the fence regarding the application of the theory of guilt when referring to an obligation of result.

First, we want to position ourselves against such change and this objective responsibility in general and should analyze the specific case. The human being, biological and spiritual being, can never be treated as an object, as a product that, presenting defect, must be exchanged or indemnified.

As we had the opportunity to participate in symposia, as mentioned during the work, the medical class has even been striving to demonstrate and clarify to the legal class that the human body is very complex and biological responses to surgical or aesthetic interventions can bring a positive or negative result.

As in the case of cosmetic surgery and reparative surgeries, there may be scars by tissue reactions of each organism, which in itself is not a proof that can be given an objective character, determining compensation, without analyzing the concrete case and all the details of the treatment.

As was commented in the present study, specialties considered as obligations of medium and result can change, taking into account the form of hiring and the patient's physical state.

A patient who wants to make a whitening, for example, is behind a better aesthetic and expects a result. Now, if he presents periodontal problems, with gingival involvement, that is, bleeding and sensitivity, and still wants to do the bleaching, it would no longer be an obligation of result due to the physical conditions present.

Although the dentist's responsibility is generally contractual, it should be analyzed whether the professional assured the patient of a result, as in cases where computer resources are used to see the before and after an aesthetic treatment. In this case, it responds objectively. Otherwise, even in cases where a result is expected, such as a fixed anterior prosthesis, if the professional warns the patient of the possibility of the final result not being satisfactory due to several factors such as periodontal problems, bone resorptions, etc., the obligation is medium, as is in large part of dental treatments.

As mentioned earlier, some specialties are related to characteristics of the obligation of medium and result, as the case may be.

Within the various dental specialties, if the professional calls himself a specialist without being, this is one of the main factors that led the patient to choose him; in the case of accountability, we understand that it can be objective, as the case may be. Article 36 of Resolution No. 185/93 of the Federal Council of Dentistry says that only suitably qualified people can qualify as specialists, and Article 39 lists existing specialties. The Code of Ethics also prohibits the title of an expert without registration in the Regional Council.

We understand that in the case of dental error, the specialist should be charged more accurately than the general practitioner because his name was one of the main factors of choice of the patient, and also, the price charged is higher, compatible with the expectation of those who seek it.

Some authors defend the need to regulate the dentist's activity and limits of action. Still, it would be challenging to place in a standard all the numerous biological factors and particularities of each specific case.

There are treatments such as endodontics that the simple lack of the patient to a session can compromise the final result of treatment or the non-ingestion of the medication at the correct time, which would be difficult to ascertain to prove the patient's guilt in the event of treatment failure.

If there is a risk to be at risk, it is necessary to count on the patient's informed consent, only dispensable in case of urgency. If this does not occur, the dentist may answer for the aggravating factors resulting from the procedure.

Radiographs appear in almost all judicial proceedings as proof of excellent material value and must be stored; the importance of radiographs as a basis for procedures performed is invaluable.

The dentist should only act within the approved procedures within the profession. Furthermore, the Brazilian Constitution and international organizations protected the right to health, making the Direito increasingly interested in the medical sciences, including dentistry. Nevertheless, the dentist has risks in exercising his professional activity, and if requested, they must prove in court that they have acted correctly.

Dental professionals must know the Consumer Protection Code and personal responsibility. However, the dentist's performance, as mentioned, should be analyzed under two distinct situations: when it is proposed to carry out some intervention, whose obligation is assumed as a result, such as an aesthetic restoration, from the one where only § 4 of art. 14 of the CDC would apply, as when the dentist proposed to make some intervention whose obligation is of means, such as surgery, adopting personal responsibility, by verifying the existence of guilt.

We are moving towards a very formal relationship between the professional and the patient, a genuine consumption relationship. The dentist has not yet become aware that he works in a segment of the society that is very informed about their rights, including consumer rights.

We believe that many professionals are not prepared for the Consumer Protection Code because the vast majority of dentists have not documented themselves correctly. In the face of a lawsuit, they could hardly prove everything that was done or not done. It would be difficult to confirm the patient's authorization and even how much their collaboration influenced treatment failure, if applicable.

In the face of the above, it is up to the dentist to document himself to refute any unfounded claims by the consumer because the CDC provides for the reversal of the burden of proof in favor of the consumer.

The challenge to allegations of professional misconduct must be firmly based on the documents the dental records. It is essential that this understanding be considered when dental-legal documents are produced due to professional care.

Proper documentation is necessary to prevent possible actions by consumers, who have the right to plead for civil compensation for the damage. According to Art. 206, § 3, V, CC, they have three years from the date of the fact and its authorship.

Because they do not have this legal conscience, they despise the custody of quality documents while guarding useless documents. Of course, it will be challenging when producing evidence in numerous cases, and most of it does not care about the law.

Many dentists get out of patients' medical records before the legal period of prescription for repair damages has elapsed. It usually does not leave the patient's signature. As a result, they are generally unaware of the principal aspects of the CDC about the profession and the specific laws of dentistry.

It is of great value to enter into a written and signed contract where both parties agree on what has been proposed so that at the end of the treatment, everything is stipulated to be compared with the final result of the same.

The dentist, the oral health professional, deals with the human being as a whole, who often arrives at the office seeking to restore his self-esteem, dealing with psychological aspects, and the success of the treatment depends significantly on the collaboration of the patient.

In endodontic treatment, one deals a lot with pain. In orthodontic treatment, the patient should collaborate with hygiene, and the older the adult patient is, the tendency to be more challenging to adapt.

We must keep in mind that the profession of a dentist is complex, where each new concrete case is a new challenge, dealing with various biological factors such as the health of the body as a whole, bacteria, the invasive power of viruses, and so many other aspects of this complex machine that is the human body, and even the influence of the stress of modern life, such as patients affected by bruxism, grinding their teeth and making an extreme force, impairing the success of treatment, both orthodontic, endodontic or even in the restoring dentistry.

It is interesting how the health professional, the dentist, having the role of relieving pain, who spends several hours of the day working on his health, when dealing with patients who can carry various diseases and even physical exhaustion, performing services often standing, performing several radiographs daily, and for that very part, having a retirement with five years less of service, be placed at all times in the dock.

You should keep in mind, in case a patient attends the office with a tooth already well damaged, protect himself from radiographic documentation, contracts, and statements that warn the patient of the prognosis of failure of treatment, because indeed, if not successful, it will have to face a process, however well-intentioned it may be.

We seek the awareness of dental professionals of their civil liability and clarifications of professionals from the legal world about the details of a biological system, how we are, and the social implications of the dentist's activity.

We wanted to demonstrate that obtaining appropriate treatments simply by punishing laws will not achieve the goal of better dentistry, or rather, preparing professionals for fear of lawsuits, but awareness on the part of dentists, the legal aspects of their profession, as well as the legal world, socio-economic aspects of the dentist's profession and the conditions of the patients who seek them. Just as in the legal world, there are cases and cases, in dentistry, it is also not able to say that there is the damage should be punished.

The use of empirical research made in the field in Juizado was complemented by the theoretical, leading us to these final considerations. Because of the end of the dentist, which is the preservation of a perfect smile and transmitting the joy of living, it is essential to clarify to the professionals the subject laws and the reality of dentistry in Brazil so that judges and society, in general, can also judge professionals with the objective measure, of the world we are currently living in.

All these are factors that influence the final result, not only depending on a relationship of consumption, as a commodity, a product, because in addition to the human being the most complex work of the Creator, man is still in the first steps in search of this level of perfection. Therefore, trying to imitate both in aesthetics, as the dentist when dealing with the smile, as in judgments, when a man takes the place of God, trying to do justice is complex. In specific cases, they cannot, for only the Father is given the understanding of the whole, both of the physical and the spiritual.

REFERENCES

ACQUAVIVA, M.C. – **Vademecum Universitário de Direito**. São Paulo: Ed. Jurídica Brasileira, 1999 – 2.a ed.

AGUIAR JÚNIOR, Ruy Rosado de. **Responsabilidade Civil do Médico**. Revista dos Tribunais, São Paulo, v. 718, p. 33-53, ago. 1995.

ARBENZ, Guilherme Oswaldo. Responsabilidade profissional do cirurgião-dentista. In: FRANÇA, Beatriz Helena Sottile. **Responsabilidade Civil e Criminal do Cirurgião-Dentista**. 1993. Tese (Mestrado em Odontologia Legal e Deontologia) – Faculdade de Odontologia, Universidade Estadual de Campinas, Piracicaba.

BASTOS, Celso Ribeiro, 1938 – **Curso de direito constitucional** – 22. ed. Atual. – São Paulo: Saraiva, 2001.

BAÚ, Marilise Kostelnaki. **O contrato de assistência médica e a responsabilidade civil**. Ed. Forense. São Paulo, 2. ed., 2001.

BENJAMIN, AHV. **Comentários ao Código do Consumidor**. São Paulo: Saraiva, 1991.

BENNET, John C.. **As Mecânicas do Tratamento ortodôntico e o Aparelho Pré-Ajustado**. Inglaterra. Ed. Artes Médicas, 1994.

BEVILÁQUA, C. **Código civil dos Estados Unidos do Brasil comentado**. Rio de Janeiro: Ed. Rio, 1958.

BIERWAGEN, Mônica Yoshiza. **Breves comentários sobre o nexo causal nos eventos de causalidade múltipla**. São Paulo, 2002. Disponível em: <http://www.editoraforense.com.br>. Acesso em 10 out 2002.

BITTAR, C. A – **Responsabilidade civil médica, odontológica e hospitalar**. São Paulo: Ed.Saraiva, 1991.

BRANCO, Gerson Luiz Carlos. **Aspectos da Responsabilidade Civil e do Dano Médico.** Revista dos Tribunais, São Paulo, v. 733, p. 53-75, nov. 1996.

BRASIL. Constituição (1988) .**Constituição da República Federativa do Brasil**. Brasília, DF.

BRASIL.Constituição (1988). **Constituição da República Federativa do Brasil.** São Paulo. Ed. RT, 1996.

BRASIL. 1990. Presidência da República. Lei nº 8.080 de 19/09/1990. **Lei Orgânica da Saúde.**

BRUNO, Aníbal. **Direito Penal – Parte Geral – VI.** Rio de Janeiro: Forense, 2ª ed., 1978.

CAHALI, Yussef Said. **Dano Moral**. 2ª ed. São Paulo: Saraiva, 1998.

CALVIELLI, I.T.P. – **O Exercício Ilegal da Odontologia no Brasil**, 1993. Tese (Mestrado em Direito). Faculdade de Direito, Universidade de São Paulo, São Paulo.

_____ O Código de Defesa do Consumidor e o Cirurgião- Dentista como prestador de Serviços. *In*: SILVA, M. **Compêndio de Odontologia Legal**. São Paulo. Medsi, 1997.

CÓDIGO DE ETICA ODONTOLÓGICO . Resolução CFO 179/91, de 19/1/91. Conselho Federal de Odontologia, Rio de Janeiro.

COHEN, S.; SCHWARTZ, S. **Endodontic complication, and the law.** J. Endodontics. V. 13, n.4, Apr. 1989.

CRETELA, Júnior, J. **Comentários à Constituição de 1988**, vol.I, 2ª edição. Rio de Janeiro: Forense, 1988.

CROCE, D. e col. – **Erro Médico e o Direito** – São Paulo: Ed. Oliveira Mendes, 1997.

CUNHA, Alexandre Sanches. **Todas as constituições brasileiras**. Campinas: Bookseller, 2001.

DANTAS, Eduardo Vasconcelos dos Santos. **O seguro de responsabilidade civil e profissional.A falsa profilaxia do erro médico.** In: Jus Navigandi, n. 54. Disponível em:<http://www.jus.com.br/doutrina/texto.asp?id=2645>, acesso em 20 mai 2002.

DARUGE, E. ; MASSINI, N. Responsabilidade profissional do Cirurgião-Dentista em relação à lei civil e penal. In: **Direitos profissionais na Odontologia**. São Paulo: Ed. Saraiva, 1978

DIAS ,José de Aguiar. **Da Responsabilidade Civil**. 10.ed. Rio de Janeiro: Forense,1995. v.II.

DINIZ, Maria Helena. **Curso de direito civil brasileiro**. 9. ed. São Paulo: Saraiva, v. III, p. 42, 1994.

DIREITO, Carlos Augusto. **Responsabilidade médica nas cirurgias estéticas**, *In*:<www.solar.com.br/~amatra/carlosgustavo_1.html>. Acesso em 20 out 2002.

FARAH, E.E. – **Responsabilidade Civil – Guia prático para dentistas, médicos e profissionais de saúde**. São Paulo: QUEST – consultoria e treinamento, 1.a ed. 1998.

FRANÇA, Beatriz Helena Sottile. **Responsabilidade Civil e Criminal do Cirurgião-Dentista**. 1993. Tese (Mestrado em Odontologia Legal e Deontologia). Faculdade de Odontologia, Universidade Estadual de Campinas, Piracicaba.

_____ **O seguro de Responsabilidade Civil Profissional do Cirurgião-Dentista**. 1998. Tese (Doutorado em Odontologia Legal e Deontologia). Faculdade de Odontologia. Universidade Estadual de Campinas, Piracicaba.

FRANÇA, Genival Veloso de. **Direito Médico**. 6. ed. São Paulo : Fundo Editorial BYK-Procienx, 1994.
_____. **Medicina Legal**. 5.ed. Ed. Guanabara Koogan. Rio de Janeiro, 1995.

FREITAS, M.R. et al. **Movimentação ortodôntica-revisão da literatura. Considerações clínica e apresentação de um caso clínico.** Ortod. V.18, n.2, jul/dez. 1985.

GONÇALVES, Carlos Roberto. **Responsabilidade Civil**. 8. ed. São Paulo: Saraiva, 2003.

GOMES, Julio Cezar Meirelles; FRANÇA, Genival Veloso de. **Erro Médico – Um Enfoque Sobre Sua Origem E Suas Conseqüências.** Montes Claros (MG): Unimontes, 1999.

GOMES, 0. **Contratos**.7ª edição. Rio de janeiro: Forense, 1979.

INGLE, John I. **Êxitos y fracassos em Endodoncia**. Rer. Assoc. Odont. Arg. V. 50, n.2, 1962.

JORNAL DA APCD. **Denúncias devem mudar o panorama odontológico**. p.20-21.Fev.1994.

KRUGER, Gustav O . **Cirurgia Bucal e Maxilo-Facial**. Rio de Janeiro. Ed. Guanabara Koogan, 1984 – 5ª ed.

KFOURI NETO, Miguel, **Responsabilidade Civil do Médico**. São Paulo: Ed. Revista dos Tribunais: 3ª edição revista e ampliada, 1999;

_____**Culpa Médica e ônus da prova** – São Paulo : Editora Revista dos Tribunais, 2002.

LEONARDO, Mário Roberto. **Endodontia: tratamento de Canais Radiculares**. São Paulo. Ed. Panamericana, 1982.

LIMA, Gilberto Baumann de. **Culpabilidade do Médico e a "Lex Artis"**, *in* RT 695/427.

LOPES, Maurício Antonio Ribeiro. **Constituição da República Federativa do Brasil**. São Paulo: Editora Revista dos Tribunais, 1996.

LUTZ, Gualter Adolpho. **Erros e Acidentes em Odontologia**. Rio de Janeiro. Ed. Est. De Artes Graph.1938.

MARQUES, Fernando de Oliveira. **Código de Defesa do Consumidor**. São Paulo, RT: 2000.

MEIRELLES, HL. **Mandado de Segurança, Ação Popular e Ação Civil Publica**; 11º edição, São Paulo: Editora Revista dos Tribunais, 1987.

MONTEIRO. Washington de Barros. **Curso de Direito Civil – v. 4 – Obrigações – 1ª Parte**. São Paulo: Saraiva, 1997.

MOYERS, Robert. **Ortodontia**. Rio de Janeiro: Guanabara Koogan. 1979.

NEGRÃO, Theotonio. **Código de processo civil e legislação processual em vigor**. 28.ed. São Paulo: Saraiva, 1997.

NERY JÚNIOR. **Os princípios gerais do código brasileiro de defesa do consumidor**. São Paulo, v.3, p. 44-77,1992.

OLIVEIRA, Marcelo L.L. **Responsabilidade Civil Odontológica**. Belo Horizonte: Del Rey, 2000.

PAIVA, J.G.; ANTONIAZZI, J.H. **Endodontia: Bases para a prática clínica**. São Paulo: Artes Médicas. 1988. cap. 28.

PEREIRA, Caio Mário da Silva. **Responsabilidade Civil**. Rio de Janeiro: Ed. Forense, 1989.

PETRELLI, Eros. **Ortodontia Contemporânea**. São Paulo: Sarvier, 1988.

PIERANGELI, José Henrique. **Códigos penais do Brasil: evolução histórica**. 2.ed.São Paulo:Editora Revista dos Tribunais, 2001.

PRONTUÁRIO ODONTOLOGICO. Portaria CFO 174/92, de 07/12/92, Conselho Federal de Odontologia, Rio de Janeiro.

PRUX, Oscar Ivan. **Responsabilidade Civil do Profissional Liberal no Código de Defesa do Consumidor**. Belo Horizonte: Del Rey, 1998.

RADICCHI, Ronaldo. **Responsabilidade Civil e Criminal do Atendimento Odontológico ao Paciente HIV soropositivo**. 2001. Tese (Mestrado em Odontologia) – Faculdade de Odontologia, Universidade Estadual de Campinas, Piracicaba.

RODRIGUES, Sílvio. **Direito Civil**. V.4. Responsabilidade civil. 18. ed. São Paulo: Saraiva, p.11, 2001.

ROMANELLO NETO, Jerônimo. **Responsabilidade Civil dos Médicos**. São Paulo: Ed. Jurídica Brasileira: 1998.

ROMANI, Nello Francisco e outros. **Atlas de Técnica Endodôntica**. São Paulo. Ed. Panamed, 1986.

ROSENTHAL, Elias. **A odontologia no Brasil. História**. São Paulo. Disponível em:<http://www.geocities.com/athens/837/historia.html>. Acesso em 15 de agosto de 2003.

SAAD, Eduardo Gabriel. **Consolidação das Leis do Trabalho Comentada**. São Paulo. Ed. LTr. 29.ed., 1996.

SAMPAIO, Rogério Marrone de Castro. **Direito Civil – Responsabilidade Civil**. São Paulo: Atlas, 2000.

SÃO PAULO (Estado) . Gabinete do Secretário de Saúde. Resolução SS-15 de 18/01/1999. **Aprova Norma Técnica que estabelece condições para instalação e funcionamento de estabelecimentos de assistência odontológica, e dá outras providências**. Diário Oficial do Estado de São Paulo, São Paulo, v. 109, n.13, Poder Executivo, Seção I, 20 jan. 1999.

SHILLINGBURG, Herbert T., Jr. E outros. **Fundamentos dos Preparos Dentários**. Alemanha. Ed. Quintessence, 1ª ed. 1988.

SILVA, De Plácido e . **Vocabulário Jurídico**. Rio de Janeiro, 1998. Editora Forense.

SILVA, M.S. **Compêndio de Odontologia Legal** : Ed. Médica e Científica Ltda, 1997.

_____ Documentação em Odontologia e sua Importância Jurídica. **Odontologia e Sociedade**, São Paulo, v.1, n.1/2, p.1-3. 1999.

SILVEIRA, Reynaldo Andrade da. **Responsabilidade Civil do Médico**. Revista dos Tribunais, São Paulo, v. 674, p. 57-62, dez. 1991.

SIMPÓSIO SOBRE RESPOSNABILIDADE CIVIL E CRIMINAL DO MÉDICO. 2002 Campinas – São Paulo. Participantes: Miguel Kfouri Neto, Antonio Carlos Mathias Coltro, Heitor Regina, Sebastião Araújo, Allan Zimermmann, entre outros.

SOUZA, Néri Tadeu Câmara. **Responsabilidade civil no erro médico**. Disponível em:<http: // www.conjur.uol.com.br/textos/17106/geocities.com/odontoufpr/historia.html>. Acesso em 30 Ago 2003.

STOCO, Rui. **Iatrogenia e Responsabilidade Civil do Médico**. *in* RT 784/105;

_____ **Responsabilidade Civil e sua interpretação jurisprudencial**. 4ª ed. São Paulo: Revista dos Tribunais, 1999.

TAMBURUS, J.R. **Pesquisa radiográfica dos sucessos e insucessos do tratamento endodôntico.** In: Revista da. Associação Paulista de Cirurgiões Dentistas. V. 37, n.1, jan/fev. 1983.

TAMOTO, M. ;GUERRA, L. ; DARUGE, **O Cirurgião Dentista e o Código de Defesa do Consumidor** .Disponível em:<www.ibemol.com.br>.Acesso em 30 Ago 2002.

TAPAI, Giselle de Melo Braga . **Novo Código civil brasileiro**. Editora Revista dos Tribunais, 2002.

TEPEDINO, Gustavo . **Temas de Direito Civil**. Rio de Janeiro. Ed. Renovar. 2. ed., 2001.

VENOSA, Sílvio de Salvo. **Direito civil: responsabilidade civil**. 3. ed. São Paulo: Atlas, 2003.

WALD, Arnoldo. **Curso de Direito Civil Brasileiro – Obrigações e Contratos**. São Paulo: RT, 2000.

_____ **Curso de Direito Civil Brasileiro,** vol. II, 16ª edição, São Paulo: Editora Revista dos Tribunais, 1983.

_____ in **Dano moral no direito brasileiro**. Disponível em: <www.teiajuridica.com.br> . Acesso em 29 de novembro de 2000.

VOCABULARY

alveolar - referring to the bone cavity where the tooth is lodged.

anamnesis - initial clinical examination where the general health conditions of the patient are investigated.

angioma – tumor caused by the proliferation of blood or lymphatic vessels.

bruxism – it is the grinding of teeth, usually unconscious, that occurs more in the night when it is sleeping and causes the wear of the teeth.

calcification – is the closure of the conduit from the internal canal to the tooth due to the deposition of mineral salts inside it through time.

cariogenic - is what has the potential to cause cavities in the teeth.

cemento – bone structure that covers the root of the teeth.

cementoblasts – biological structures responsible for the formation of the root of teeth.

cements – calcification of the elements of connection of the tooth with the bone, becoming cemented in the bone, with difficult removal.

endodontics - dental specialty that deals with the channels of teeth.

stomatognathic - digestive system of the human body.

extraction - tooth extraction.

extraction - removal of a dental element.

hypoplasia – underdevelopment of an organ by effect of reduction of cell proliferation.

fibromucosa – tissue that covers the oral cavity in its inner part.

phleimon - inflammation of subcutaneous and subaponeurotic connective tissue.

fluorosis - color change caused in the teeth due to excess fluoride in the water.

forceps - dental instrument used to make dental extractions.

homeostasis – state of equilibrium of the living organism in relation to its various functions and the chemical composition of its fluids and tissues.

idiopathic disease that is not a consequence of another.

impacted - occluded, prevented from moving.

intrusion – occurs when the tooth moves into the alveolo, with its crown at a lower height than the adjacent teeth.

maintainers – maintain the space of deciduous teeth or milk after their loss, aiming at maintaining the space for the future hatching of permanent teeth.

orthodontics - dental specialty that corrects dental positioning.

orthognata - relative to the correct positioning of the jaws.

osteo-myelitis – is a type of tumor that happens in the mandibular and maxillary bones, causing its destruction.

paraesthesia – nerve disorder characterized by abnormal sensations and sensory hallucinations, such as lack of sensitivity on one side of the face.

periodontics – dental specialty that takes care of the periodontoe; of the membranes surrounding the tooth.

pericemento – membranes that surround the tooth and that serve to secure it to the bone.

prognosis - judgment of the development of a disease based on diagnosis.

protruded – the mandible is presented in an advanced plane in relation to the maxilla.

pulpitis - acute pain of the dental element, due to deterioration of the pulp that exists within it.

retruded – the mandible is in a retrograde position in relation to the jaw.

sealant – is a type of resin that is placed in the teeth to prevent the appearance of cavities.

syncope - sudden drop in pressure or circulatory collapse, accompanied by cerebral anemia and loss of consciousness.

tartar – common name that is given to the calculation, which is the accumulation of dirt, mineral salts and bacteria that form around the limit of the tooth with the gum.

trepanation - act of drilling. In endodontics is the act of drilling the canal, compromising its integrity, causing the possible loss of it.

trismus - involuntary closure of the mouth resulting from spasmodic contraction of the elevator muscles of the lower jaw.

ANEXO OF LEGISLATION

A - Federal Constitution

THEMATIC INDEX OF THE FEDERAL CONSTITUTION - 1988

CONSUMER

Defense - CF art. 5, XXXII, and art. 170, V

Rights; Public Services - CF art. 175, single paragraph, II

Responsibility for Damage Ao; Competing Legislation - CF art. 24, VIII

single health system - CF art. 200, I

TITLE II

Fundamental Rights and Guarantees

CHAPTER I

INDIVIDUAL AND COLLECTIVE RIGHTS AND DUTIES

Article 5 ° All are equal before the law, without distinction of any nature, guaranteeing brazilians and foreigners residing in the country the inviolability of the right to life, liberty, equality, security and property, in the following terms:

XXXII - the State will promote, in the form of the law, consumer protection;

Art. 24. It is up to the Union, the States and the Federal District to legislate concurrently on:

XII - social security, protection and defense of health;

Title VII

Of the Economic and Financial Order

CHAPTER I

OF THE GENERAL PRINCIPLES OF ECONOMIC ACTIVITY

Art. 170. The economic order, founded on the valorization of human work and free initiative, aims to assure everyone a dignified existence, according to the dictates of social justice, observed the following principles:

V - consumer protection;

Art. 175. It is the responsibility of the Public Power, in the form of the law, directly or under concession or permission regime, always through bidding, the provision of public services.

Single paragraph. The law will provide for:

II - the rights of users;

HEALTH

Shares and services of - CF art. 198

Assistance to; foreign companies or capital; participation - CF art. 199, § 3

Assistance to; private initiative; free participation - CF art. 199, caput

Child and adolescent assistance - CF art. 227, § 1

Maternal and child care; appeals - CF art. 227, § 1, I

Common competence of the Union, States, Federal District and Municipalities - CF art. 23, II

Law of all and duty of the State - CF art. 196

Private institution; public resources - CF art. 199, § 2

Municipalities; customer service - CF art. 30, VII

Protection and defense; competing legislation - CF art. 24, XII

Social security; entitlement - CF art. 194

Work; protection standard - CF art. 7, XXII

Human organ transplantation; blood transfusion - CF art. 199, § 4

UNIFIED HEALTH SYSTEM

Food, beverages and water; supervision - CF art. 200, VI

Competence - CF art. 200

Constitution, organization and financing CF art. 198

Scientific and technological development; increment - CF art. 200, V

Private institutions; participation - CF art. 199, § 1

Medicines, equipment, immunobiologicals and blood products; production -CF art. 200, I

Environment; protection - CF art. 200, VIII

Products, substances and procedures - health; control and supervision - CF art. 200, I

Psychoactive, toxic and radioactive products; control and supervision - CF art. 200, VII

Human resources; training - CF art. 200, III

Basic sanitation; participation - CF art. 200, IV

Health, epidemiological and health surveillance - CF art. 200, II

Section II

HEALTH

Art. 196. Health is the right of all and the duty of the State, guaranteed through social and economic policies aimed at reducing the risk of disease and other injuries and universal and equal access to actions and services for its promotion, protection and recovery.

Art. 197. Health actions and services are of public relevance, and it is up to the Government to have, in accordance with the law, on its regulation, supervision and control, and its execution must be done directly or through third parties and also by a natural or legal person under private law.

Art. 198. Public health actions and services are part of a regionalized and hierarchical network and constitute a single system, organized according to the following guidelines:

I - decentralization, with a single direction in each sphere of government;

II - comprehensive care, with priority for preventive activities, without prejudice to care services;

III - community participation.

(*) § 1st Single Paragraph. The single health system will be financed, in accordance with art. 195, with resources from the social security budget, the Union, the States, the Federal District and the Municipalities, as well as other sources. (*) Single paragraph amended to § 1 by Constitutional Amendment No. 29 of 09/13/00:

Paragraph included by Constitutional Amendment No. 29 of 13/09/00:

"§ 2º The Union, the States, the Federal District and the Municipalities shall apply, annually, in actions and public health services minimum resources derived from the application of percentages calculated on:" (CA)

"I – in the case of the Union, in the form defined in accordance with the supplementary law provided for in Paragraph 3;" (AC)

"II – in the case of the States and the Federal District, the proceeds of the collection of taxes referred to in Art. 155 and the resources of which the arts are treated. 157 and 159, item I(a) and item II, minus the parcels which are transferred to the respective municipalities;" (AC)

"III – in the case of the Municipalities and the Federal District, the proceeds of the collection of taxes referred to in Art. 156 and the resources of which the arts are treated. 158 and 159, item I, point (b) and § 3." (AC)

Paragraph included by Constitutional Amendment No. 29 of 13/09/00:

"§ 3rd Supplementary law, which will be reevaluated at least every five years, will establish:" (AC)

"I - the percentages of which § 2 is treated;" (AC)

"II – the criteria for apportionment of Union resources linked to health for states, the Federal District and municipalities, and states destined to their respective municipalities, aiming at the progressive reduction of regional disparities;" (AC)

"III – the rules for the supervision, evaluation and control of health expenditures at the federal, state, district and municipal levels;" (AC)

"IV - the rules for calculating the amount to be applied by the Union." (AC)

Art. 199. Health care is free to private initiative.

§ 1 - Private institutions may participate in a complementary way of the unified health system, according to its guidelines, by means of a public law contract or agreement, with preference to philanthropic and non-profit entities.

§ 2 - The allocation of public resources for aid or grants to private for-profit institutions is closed.

§ 3 - The direct or indirect participation of foreign companies or capital is closed

health care in the country, except in the cases provided for by law.

§ 4 - The law shall provide for the conditions and requirements that facilitate the removal of organs, tissues and human substances for the purposes of transplantation, research and treatment, as well as the collection, processing and transfusion of blood and its derivatives, and all types of commercialization are prohibited.

Art. 200. The single health system is responsible, in addition to other attributions, under the law:

I - control and supervise procedures, products and substances of interest to health and participate in the production of medicines, equipment, immunobiologicals, blood products and other substances;

II - to carry out health and epidemiological surveillance actions, as well as workers' health;

III - order the training of human resources in the health area;

IV - participate in the formulation of the policy and the implementation of basic sanitation actions;

V - to increase in its area of activity the scientific and technological development;

VI - inspect and inspect food, including the control of their nutritional content, as well as beverages and waters for human consumption;

VII - participate in the control and supervision of the production, transportation, custody and use of psychoactive, toxic and radioactive substances and products;

VIII - to collaborate in the protection of the environment, understood in work.

B - Law 5,081 of August 24, 1966

Regulates the Exercise of Dentistry.

THE PRESIDENT OF THE REPUBLIC:

I make it known that the National Congress decrees and I sanction the following Law:

Art. 1 - The exercise of dentistry in the national territory is governed by the provisions of this Law.

Art. 2 - The exercise of Dentistry in the national territory is only allowed to the dentist qualified by school or college official or recognized, after the registration of the diploma in the Board of Higher Education, in the National Service of Supervision of Dentistry, under whose jurisdiction the place of its activity is found.

Single paragraph. (Vetoed).

Art. 3 - Dentistry in the national territory may be those qualified by foreign schools, after the revalidation of the diploma and meeting the other requirements of the previous article.

Art. 4 - The right to the exercise of dentistry is guaranteed, with legal restrictions, to the graduate under the conditions mentioned in Decree-Law Number 7,718 of 9 of July 1945, which regularly qualified for professional practice, only within the territorial boundaries of the State where the school or college that graduated operated operated.

Art. 5 - Any administrative authorization is null and void to those who are not legally qualified for the exercise of dentistry.

Art. 6 - The dentist is responsible for:

I - practice all acts pertinent to Dentistry, arising from knowledge acquired in regular course or in postgraduate courses;

II - prescribe and apply pharmaceutical specialties for internal and external use, indicated in Dentistry;

III - to attest, in the sector of his professional activity, morbid states and others, including, to justify absences from employment;

IV - to carry out the dental expertise in civil, criminal, labor and administrative forum;

V - apply local and tronce anesthesia;

VI - use analgesia and hypnosis, as long as proven enabled, when they constitute effective means for treatment.

VII - maintain, attached to the office, prosthesis laboratory, equipment and installation suitable for clinical research and analysis, related to specific cases of its specialty, as well as X-ray devices, for diagnosis, and physiotherapy equipment;

VIII - prescribe and apply urgent medication in the case of serious accidents that compromise the patient's life and health;

IX - use, in the exercise of the function of perito-dentist, in cases of necropsy, the access routes of the neck and head.

Art. 7 - The dentist is sealed:

a) to publicly display dental work and use propaganda devices to raise customers;

b) announce cure of certain diseases, for which there is no effective treatment;

c) exercise of more than two specialties;

(d) consultations by correspondence, radio, television, or similar means;

e) provision of free service in private offices;

f) disclose benefits received from customers;

g) announce prices of services, payment modalities and other forms of commercialization of the clinic that mean unfair competition.

Art. 8 - (Vetoed).

I - (Vetted).

II - (Vetoed).

Art. 9 - (Vetoed).

a) (Vetted);

b) (Vetted);

(c) (Vetoed);

d) (Vetted);

e) (Vetoed).

Art. 10 - (Vetoed).

Single paragraph. (Vetoed).

Art. 11 - (Vetoed).

Art. 12 - The Executive Branch will lower Decree, within 90 (ninety)

days, regulating this Law.

Art. 13 - This Law will enter into force on the date of its publication, repealed Decree-Law Number 7,718 of July 9, 1945, Law No. 1,314 of January 17, 1951, and other provisions to the contrary.

Brasilia, August 24, 1966; 145th of independence and 78th of the Republic.

C - Resolution No. 185 of 26 April 1993

Title I

From the legal exercise of consolidation the rules for procedures in dentistry councils

Title I

Legal exercise

Chapter I - Preliminary Provisions

Art. 1. They are obliged to register with the Federal Council and to register with the Regional Councils of Dentistry in whose jurisdiction they are established or perform their activities:

a) dentists;b) dental technicians; c) dental hygiene technicians;d) dental office attendants;e) dental assistants;f) specialists, provided that this is announced or titled;g) the dental care providers;h) dental laboratories;i) other professional assistants who may have their occupations regulated;j) the activities that may be, in any form, linked to the Dental Councils.

Single paragraph. Registration and registration in two or more professional categories are closed in the Federal and Regional Councils of Dentistry without the presentation of the respective diplomas or certificates of completion of a regular vocational course.

Art. 2. The Federal and Regional Councils will, mandatorily, in the proceedings under investigation, a maximum period of 90 (ninety) days, to comply with their requirements.

§ 1. If the interested parties do not meet the requirements within the established deadlines, the claim should be rejected and the case filed.

§ 2. The process may only be unfiled upon specific requirement and recollection of fees.

Art. 3. Only individuals and legal entities that meet the minimum requirements set out in these standards may be deferred.

Chapter II

Private Activities of the Dentist

Art. 4. The exercise of the private professional activities of the dentist is only permitted with compliance with the provisions of Laws 4.324, de 14.04.64 and 5.081, of 08.24.66, in Decree No. 68,704, of 03.06.71; and, in these norms.

§ 1. It is up to the dentist:

I - practice all acts relevant to dentistry arising from knowledge acquired in regular course or in postgraduate courses;

II - prescribe and apply pharmaceutical specialties for internal and external use, indicated in Dentistry;

III - to attest, in the sector of their professional activity, morbid states and others, including to justify lack of employment;

IV - to carry out the dental expertise in civil, criminal, labor and administrative forum;

V - apply local and troncular anesthesia;

VI - to use analgesia and hypnosis, provided proven qualified, when they constitute effective means for treatment;

VII - maintain, attached to the office, prosthesis laboratory, equipment and installation suitable for clinical research and analysis, related to specific cases of its specialty, as well as X-ray devices, for diagnosis, and physiotherapy equipment;

VIII - prescribe and apply urgent medication in the case of serious accidents that compromise the patient's life and health;

IX - use, in the exercise of the function of dental expert, in cases of necropsy, the access routes of the neck and head.

§ 2. The dentist may operate patients submitted to any of the means of general anesthesia, provided that the recommended precautionary requirements for their use are met.

§ 3. The dentist can only perform professional work on patients under general anesthesia when it is performed by a specialist medical professional and in a hospital environment that has the necessary conditions common to surgical environments.

§ 4. The rights and duties of the dentist, as well as what is sealed to him, are explained in the Code of Dental Ethics.

§ 5. It is allowed to the announcement of agreements maintained between dental clinic and entities, in keeping with the provisions of the CEO.

§ 6. The following forms of service may appear on printed, plates, or advertisements:

a) home care; and

b) care to special patients.

§ 7. The use of the terms "prevention" and "rehabilitation" is allowed to any dentist who wishes to register and enroll his clinic, using them in the respective

Denominations.

§ 8. The dentist should require the registration number in the Regional Council to the technician in dental prosthesis in the documents presented to him, under penalty of establishing an Ethical Process.

§ 9. The dentist who, having dental hygiene technician and/or dental office attendant under his supervision, will answer ethically before the respective Regional Council, to allow them, in any form, to go out of their specific functions.

§ 10. The dentist is obliged to keep informed the respective Regional Council as to the existence, in his private practice or in a clinic under his responsibility, of an auxiliary professional.

§ 11. The information referred to in the preceding paragraph shall include the name of the assistant, the date of his admission, his profession and the number of his/her registration in the Regional Council.

Art. 5. To qualify for registration and registration, the professional must meet one of the following requirements:

a) to be graduated by dentistry course recognized by the Ministry of Education and Sports;

b) be graduated by a foreign school, whose diploma has been revalidated and/or compulsorily registered for the qualification to professional practice throughout the national territory;

c) be graduated by school or state college, which has worked with authorization from the state government, when benefited by Decree-Law 7.718, of July 9, 1945 and proven the qualification for professional practice until August 26, 1966;

d) be licensed pursuant to Decrees 20,862 of December 28, 1931; 21,703 of 22 February 1932; or 22,501 of February 27, 1933; and

e) have pasted grade less than two (2) years from the date of the application, provided that it has a declaration of the educational institution, signed by a competent authority and expressly stated, in full: name, nationality, date and place of birth, identity card number, and date of degree.

§ 1. The student's diploma agreement can only be accepted for registration and registration, when it does not contain a restrictive handout to professional practice in Brazil or has been canceled.

§ 2. In the case of point (c), professional practice shall be restricted to the territorial limits of the State where the school has functioned.

§ 3. In the case of point (d), the professional practice shall be restricted to the locality for which the licence has been issued.

§ 4. In the case provided for in point (e), the authorization for the exercise of the profession shall be for the period of 2 (two) years, counted from the date of its degree of.

§ 5. The registration and registration of professionals registered in public health agencies until April 14, 1964, may be made regardless of the presentation of the diplomas, upon certificate provided by the competent agencies.

Art. 6. You are required to register and enroll the dentist in the performance:

a) of its activity as self-employed; b) of position, function or public employment, civil or military, of the direct or indirect administration, of federal, state or municipal scope, for whose appointment, appointment, hiring, possession and exercise is required or necessary the condition of professional dentistry;c) of the teaching profession, when the exercise is depending on his diploma of dental surgeon;d) of any other activity, through employment or not, for whose exercise is indispensable the condition of dentist, or graduate of higher education, provided that, in this case, only has that qualification.

Art. 43. The dentist is restricted to the use of the infrahyoid cervical pathway, for escaping the domain of his area of activity, as well as the practice of cosmetic surgery, with the reasons for the aesthetic-functional masticatory apparatus.

Art. 44. Dentists can only perform surgeries under general anesthesia, in a hospital environment, whose technical director is a doctor, and who have the indispensable safety conditions common to surgical environments, considering ethics practice to request and/or perform general anesthesia in the office of a dentist, doctor or outpatient clinic.

Art. 45. Only surgeries that can be performed under local anesthesia can be performed in clinics or outpatient clinics.

Art. 46. Quando o êxito letal for atingido como resultado do ato cirúrgico odontológico, deverá ser o atestado de óbito fornecido pelo médico que tenha participado do ato cirúrgico ou pelo Instituto Médico Legal.

Art. 47. In cases of autogenous grafts, whose donor region is outside the bucomaxillofacial area, they should be removed by physicians.

Art. 48. In cases of diseases of the salivary glands, with expansion or involvement that reach regions outside the bucomaxillofacial area, malignant tumors of the oral cavity and neurological disorders with maxillofacial manifestations, it is essential that the dentist act integrated with the doctor.

Art. 49. In injuries of common interest to Dentistry and Medicine, referred to in the previous article, the surgical team must be constituted of a doctor and dentist, for the proper handling of the intended result, and the team is then under the head of the physician.

D - Health Code of São Paulo art. 22 to 32.

Article 22 –" Dental care establishments must present, in addition to the other obligations determined by the municipal legislation of buildings in force, the following conditions related to the area in which dental procedures will be performed:

I - Lighting that allows good visibility, without glare or shadows;
II - Ventilation that allows circulation and air renewal;
III – Coatings of floors with washable and waterproof material, which allows the processes

of decontamination and / or cleaning, without the presence of cracks, or discontinuity;

IV – Masonry walls or partitions of light color, coated with washable and waterproof material, which allows the processes of decontamination and / or cleaning, without the presence of mold or discontinuities;

V - Light-colored liners, without the presence of infiltrations, cracks or mold

VI- Hydraulic and electrical installations built-up or protected by gutters or external channels, so that there are no dirt deposits in its extension.

Article 23 – The entire establishment of dental care must have a washbasin with running water, exclusively used for hand washing of the members of the oral health team.

I – Hand washing is mandatory for all components of the oral health team.

II - The washbasin must have:

a – device that dispenses hands contact with tap or registration steering wheel when water is closed;

(b) disposable paper towels or sterile compresses;

c - liquid soap.

III – Cleaning and/or decontamination of articles should not be carried out in the same washbasin for hand washing.

Article 24 – Clinics and Modular Clinics must have equipment for sterilization compulsorily outside the service area.

OBS - Clinics : are classified as dental clinic type I and dental clinic type II.

Dental clinic type I - is the establishment of dental care characterized by having a set of, at most 03 dental offices, independent among si, com uma área de espera em comum, podendo fazer uso ou não de equipamento de Raios – X odontológico. – N.T. Artigo 9º - inciso II.

Dental clinic type II - is the establishment of dental care characterized by having a set of, at most 03 dental offices, independent of each other, with a waiting area in common, and that maintains attached, dental prosthesis laboratory, and may make use or not of dental X equipment.- N.T. Article 9 - item III.

Modular Clinic - is the establishment of dental care characterized by the care in a single space with minimum area conditioned to the number and disposal of dental equipment, being able to make use or not of dental X-ray equipment as provided in this N.T. - N.T. Article 9 - item V.

I – In polyclinics, sterilization equipment must be installed in rooms with at least two distinct areas with independent ventilation, direct to the outside and separated to the ceiling, with passage counter, without crossing flow, being an area endortized with water point, vat and bench for reception of contaminated material, purge and washing, and another for preparation, sterilization, guarding and distribution of the material.

NOTE - There are two types of Clinics defined in N.T.:

Dental polyclinic: it is the establishment of dental care characterized by a set of more than 03 dental offices, independent of each other, and may even maintain in their interior, modular clinics, dental prosthesis laboratories, radiology institute or radiological documentation. N.T. Article 9 - item VIII

Polyclinic of dental education : it is the polyclinic characterized by developing activities aimed at dental teaching or research. N.T. Article 9 - item IX.

Article 25 - In the modalities of transportable units and mobile units shall present:
I – supply of drinking water in sufficient quantity for its intended purpose, with a drinking water tank constructed of material which:
a - do not contaminate water;
b – with smooth, resistant and waterproof surface;
(c) allow easy access for inspection and cleaning;
d - enable its total exhaustion;

II - reservoir for collection of fluids from the work process developed in the unit with the following characteristics:
a - constructed with resistant material;
b - with smooth and waterproof surface;
(c) allowing easy access to inspection and cleaning;
d – which allows its total exhaustion in the public sewage system or other device approved by abnt technical standards, being mandatory its periodic cleaning and disinfection.

OBS - It is understood as:

Transportable unit: that installed in previously structured places and with temporary permanence and must, for this, present equipment adapted and appropriate to dental care. N.T. Article 10 - item II - letter a.

Mobile unit : one characterized by being installed on or by a self-propelled vehicle. N.T. Article 10 - item II - letter b.
Dental procedures, pursuant to Article 10 of the N.T. adopted by Resolution SS – 15, of January 18, 1999, may be performed in the following modalities:

Intra-establishment : those carried out within the physical area of the establishment of

dental care;

- Extra establishment: those performed outside the physical area of the dental care establishment Dental Office the use of the following units: Transportable Unit, Mobile Unit and Portable Care Unit characterized, the latter, by the care of patients with portable equipment focused mainly on cases of impossibility of locomotion of the patient, including in the cases of hospitalized patients.

WAITING AREA
Characteristics

The waiting area must be at least 10 square meters, except for the Type I and II Dental Offices whose area must have the footage compatible with the number of patients treated. This area should have the following minimum characteristics. pursuant to Article 26 of the N.T. adopted by Resolution SS - 15, of January 18, 1999:
I - provide conditions for patients to wait seated;
II - have ventilation, natural and / or artificial that allows circulation and renewal of air.
According to Article 30 of the n.t. retro cited, in the modalities of extra establishment care there is no need for a specific area for waiting for patients, however it is recommended that the space for so is sheltered and observe proximity to the care area.

SERVICE AREA

Footage

Article 27 – Dental care facilities must comply with the following minimum limits for the physical areas where procedures and waiting area will be performed:
Dental offices types I and II - 6 square meters.

OBS - Understands by:

- Dental office type I - the establishment of dental care characterized by having only a set of dental equipment, and may or may not make use of dental X-ray equipment. N.T. - Article 9 - item I.
- Dental office type II - the establishment of dental care characterized by having only one set of dental equipment, and that keeps attached, dental prosthesis laboratory, and may make use or not of dental X-ray equipment. N.T. - Article 9 - item II.

Dental clinics types I and II and Polyclinic ; 6 square meters per office installed: minimum of 10 square meters.

Modular and Polyclinic Clinic of dental education: 6 square meters per dental chair: minimum of 10 square meters.

Institute of Radiology - Institute of Dentistradiology - 6 square meters per device installed, obeying the proportion of one device per room.

Institute of Dental Documentation: 6 square meters per radiation device

ionizing installed, obeying the proportion of one appliance per room, and 6 square meters per office installed to perform the other activities.

Article 28 – All dental care facilities must be provided, in addition to the areas for dental procedures and for waiting for patients:
I - place to file;
II - place for storage and packaging of instruments and medicines.

Article 29 – In the modality of extra establishment care, there should be sufficient physical area for the installation of its equipment providing favorable working conditions to the oral health team. It is also necessary to consider what is available decree No. 12,342, of September 27, 1978 in its Articles:
Article 255 - Places for dental care, such as dental clinics (official or private) , specialized dental clinics and popular dental polyclinics, dental emergency rooms, dental and similar institutes, in addition to the requirements relating to housing and work establishments in general, shall further meet the following:
....
III – compartments provided with doors, separated to the lining by walls or uninterrupted divisions ....

Article 256 – The establishments of which this chapter is treated shall have independent entry and may not be used for other purposes, nor serve as a passage to another place.

HEALTH
NT approved by Resolution SS - 15, of 18.01.99
Article 31 – Dental care facilities of the dental office type shall have a sanitary

compartment for the public, not necessarily in the physical area delimited by the establishment, but a proximity to it.

Article 32 – Dental clinics, modular clinics, dental polyclinics, radiology institutes and dental documentation institutes shall provide for a health compartment for:
a - employees of the oral health team;
b - for the public of the establishment.

PARTITIONS

All compartments of dental care facilities bordering the service area must be separated walls or partition to the ceiling.

Annex II of Resolution SS - 15 of 18 January 1999 constitutes the Basic Roadmap for Inspection of Dental Assistance Establishments and the non-observance of any of its items implies the rejection of the Licensing and/or the application of the Notice of Infraction.

Item V - 1. requires : Service area bounded by wall or partition to the ceiling,

with its own sewer connection for each office."[121]

E - Consolidation of The Rules for Procedures in the Regional Councils - DECREE No. 68,704, FROM JUNE 3, 1971
It regulates Law No. 4,324 of April 14, 1964.

The President of the Republic, using the attribution conferred on him by Article 81, item III, of the Constitution, and in view of the provisions of Article 30 of Law No. 4,324 of April 14, 1964, decrees:

CHAPTER I

INTRODUCTION

Art. 1 - The Federal Council and the Regional Councils of Dentistry, established by Law No. 4,324 of April 14, 1964, aims to supervise professional ethics throughout the national territory, and it is up to them to ensure and work for the good concept of the profession and those who exercise it legally.
Single paragraph. It is up to the Federal and Regional Councils; also, as selection bodies, the discipline and supervision of dentistry throughout the country, the defense of the free exercise of the profession, as well as the judgment of violations of law and ethics.
Art. 2 - The Federal Council and the Regional Councils constitute, as a whole, an Autarchy, with legal personality of public law, endowed with regional councils, administrative and financial autonomy; without prejudice to subordination to the Federal Council, in the form of Law 4,324 of April 14, 1964, and this Regulation.
Single paragraph. The Municipality is bound by the Ministry of Labor and Social Security, for the purposes of Decree Law No. 968, of October 13, 1969.
Art. 3 - The Federal Council of Dentistry has as its place the capital of the Republic.

---

[121]São Paulo (Capital). Resolution SS - 15, of January 18, 1999 Approves N.T. Technical Standard. **It establishes conditions for the installation and operation of dental care establishments, and provides related measures,** 1999.

Art. 4- In each Capital of State, Territory and Federal District there will be a Regional Council of Dentistry, named according to its jurisdiction, which will reach, respectively, that of the State, the Territory and that of the Federal District.

Single paragraph. If the number of professionals in a State or Territory does not offer planning conditions for the installation of a Regional Council, the Federal Council may incorporate the professionals of the region to the Regional Council that offers better conditions of communication and assistance.

CHAPTER II

OF THE FEDERAL COUNCIL OF DENTISTRY

Art. 5 - The Federal Council of Dentistry consists of 9 (nine) effective members and equal number of alternates, with a three-year term, elected by secret ballot and a majority of votes in the assembly of delegates-electors of the Regional Councils.

Art. 6 - The mandate of the members of the Federal Council of Dentistry shall be merely honorary, requiring, as requirements for the election, the Brazilian nationality, the quality of dentist and registration in the Regional Council.

Single paragraph. The accumulation of a member of the Federal Council with that of a member of the Regional Council is deceitable.

Art. 7 - At the first ordinary meeting of the Federal Council, its Executive Board will be elected, consisting of President, Vice-President, Secretary General and Treasurer, chosen from among its effective members.

Single paragraph. Any member of the Board of Executive Officers may be replaced by a resolution of 2/3 (two-thirds) of the Council's votes, provided that the measure is proposed and approved by the Plenary.

Art. 8 - There will be the summoning of alternate in cases of impediments, removal or vacancy of effective member.

Single paragraph. The President may convene alternate to form the plenary, in case of absence or occasional impediment of the holder.

Art. 9 - The responsibilities of the Federal Council are:

(a) organise its bylaws;

b) to approve the internal rules organized by the Regional Councils;

c) to elect the Board of Directors itself;

d) vote and amend the Code of Dental Professional Ethics, after hearing the Regional Councils;

e) to promote any due diligence or verification stemming from the functioning of the Regional Councils and to adopt, where necessary, appropriate measures, including the appointment of provisional board;

f) propose to the Federal Government to amend or amend this regulation;

(g) provide the necessary instructions for the proper functioning of the Regional Councils;

(h) to become aware of any doubts raised by the Regional Councils and to resolve them;

i) in the degree of appeal, by summoning the Regional Councils or any interested party, to decide on the registration of professionals, in the Regional Councils and on penalties imposed by the said Councils;

j) proclaim the results of the elections of the members of the Federal Council for the subsequent three-year period, and the Regional Councils for the subsequent biennium;

l) apply to the members of the Regional Councils, and to themselves, the penalties that fit for the absences practiced in the exercise of their mandate;

m) to approve its own annual budget and regional councils;

n) approve, annually, the accounts of themselves and that of the Regional Councils, forwarding them, within the legal deadlines, to the Court of Auditors of the Union.

Art. 10 - The income of the Federal Council shall consist of:

a) 20% (twenty percent) of the total union contribution, paid by dentists;

(b) 1/3 (one third) of the annuities charged by the Regional Councils;

(c) 1/3 (one third) of the shipping fee for professional portfolios;

(d) 1/3 (one third) of the fines imposed by the Regional Councils;

e) donations and legacies;

(f) official grants;

g) acquired goods and values;

CHAPTER III

REGIONAL COUNCILS

Art. 11- Each Regional Council consists of 5 (five) effective members and many other alternates, with a biennial mandate, elected in a secret vote, by an absolute majority of votes of registered Dentists, in the respective region.

§ 1 - The mandate of the members of the Regional Councils of Dentistry will be merely honorary, requiring as requirements for the election, the Brazilian nationality, the status of Dentist and registration in the respective Regional Council.

§ 2º - In addition to the requirements mentioned in the 1st, the dentist who has suffered a penalty that implies the temporary suspension of the practice of the profession may not apply to a member of the Regional Council.§

Art. 12 - At the first ordinary meeting of the Regional Council, its Executive Board, composed of President, Secretary and Treasurer, shall be elected among its effective members.

Sole Paragraph - The members of the Executive Board shall be replaced, in their absences or impediments, in the manner established in their Bylaws.

Art. 13- The alternate will be summoned in cases of impediment, removal or vacancy of the effective Board Member.

Art. 14 - In case of need at the discretion of the Board, the alternates may be summoned to assist the Regional Council in the study of processes.

Sole Paragraph - Alternates may also be summoned as members of committees and participate in meetings, but do not have the right to vote.

Art. 15 - The Decision-Making Committee and the Ethics Committee shall be composed of effective and alternate Directors, and the other Committees, which may be created by the Regional Councils, may be composed of alternate Directors and Dentists duly registered in the Regional Council of jurisdiction to which they belong.

Art. 16 - The Regional Councils may designate representative in each municipality of the territory of their jurisdiction.

Art. 17- The General Assembly of each Regional Council is the registered Dentists, who find themselves in the enjoyment of their rights and even with the Treasury.

Sole Paragraph - The secondary registration does not authorize the Dentist to participate in the Assembly of the Council in which he is enrolled in this capacity.

Art. 18 - The General Assembly, led by the President of the respective Regional Council, shall meet ordinarily once a year, in the first convocation with an absolute majority of its members and, in a second convocation, with any number of members present.

§ 1st - In the year of the election of the Regional Council, the General Assembly will be held 30 to 45 days before the date set for this election.

§ 2 - The deliberations of the General Assembly shall be taken by a majority of the votes of those present.

Art. 19- The General Assembly shall be responsible for:

I- Examine and discuss the annual report and the accounts of the Board of Directors;

II - Authorize the disposal of property assets of the Council;

III - Fix or change the value of fees, fees and contributions charged by the Council;

IV- Deliberate on the issues or consultations submitted to its decision by the Board or the Board of Directors;

V- Elect a delegate and his alternate for election of the effective and alternate members of the Federal Council.

Art. 20- The Regional Councils are responsible for:

a) deliberate on registration and cancellation, in its staff, of professionals legalized;

b) supervise the practice of the profession;

c) deliberate on matters related to professional ethics, imposing on the offenders the appropriate penalties;

d) prepare its bylaws, submitting it to the approval of the Federal Council;

e) to suggest to the Federal Council the measures necessary for the regularity of the services and the supervision of the professional practice;

f) to resolve doubts regarding the competence and scope of professional activities, with suspensive appeal to the Federal Council;

g) to provide portfolios to professionals enrolled in their boards;

h) to promote, by all means at its fingertips, the perfect technical-scientific and moral performance of dentistry, the profession and those who exercise it;

i) publish annual reports of its work and the list of registered professionals;

j) to exercise acts of jurisdiction committed by law;

l) appoint a representative in each municipality of its jurisdiction;

m) submit to the approval of the Federal Council the Budget and the annual accounts.

Art. 21- The income of the Regional Councils shall consist of:

a) registration fee;

b) emoluments and contributions;

(c) 2/3 (two thirds) of the professional portfolio dispatch fee;

(d) 2/3 (two thirds) of annuities paid by professionals enrolled in the Council;

e) 2/3 (two thirds) of the fines imposed;

f) donations and legacies;

(g) official grants;

h) acquired goods and values;

§ 1 - The Regional Councils are denied the collection of any fees not expressly provided for in this article.

§ 2- The yearly fee may not be less than 30% (thirty percent) of the regional minimum wage.

CHAPTER IV

REGISTRATION WITH THE REGIONAL COUNCIL

Art. 22- Only the dental surgeon enrolled in the Regional Council of Dentistry, under whose jurisdiction his activity takes place, will be qualified to the professional practice of Dentistry.

Sole Paragraph- The exercise of private professional activities of the surgeon- requires registration in the respective Regional Council.

Art. 23 - Registration must be requested from the President of the Regional Council, with the declaration of full name, affiliation, date and place of birth, nationality, marital status, address of the residence and place of work, joining the person concerned, in addition to the title or professional certificate, identity card and, in the case of brazilian born or naturalized, discharge with military service and electoral obligations.

Sole Paragraph - The Regional Council may require the applicant to provide other information or documents, provided that it deems them necessary or indispensable for the approval of the registration.

Art. 24 - The registration of the professional will only be considered authorized after being approved at a meeting of the Regional Council, in view of the opinion of the Rapporteur Advisor, and effected after the payment of the fees due.

Sole Paragraph - The Regional Council shall register in its own book, of numbered and initialed sheets, the approved inscription, in it by releasing the number assigned to the professional and of necessary identification elements.

Art. 25 - Only the registration in the Regional Council may be granted to the professional who presents one of the following original documents:

a) Dental Surgeon's diploma registered in accordance with the legislation in force;

b) diploma of Dentist issued by foreign Faculty, revalidated and duly legalized.

c) diploma of Dentist issued by a Faculty that operated with authorization from the state government, provided that the bearer has benefited from Decree-Law No. 7,718, of July 9, 1945;

d) practical dentist's license issued by a state health agency within the deadline established in Decree No. 23,540, of December 4, 1933, provided that the permit was requested until June 30, 1934.

§ 1º- When it is a professional benefited by Decree-Law No. 7,718, of July 9, 1945, referred to in point "c" of this article, the Regional Council will make available in the professional card the impossibility of transfer to another State and, in the case of a practical dentist, referred to in point "d", the authorization to exercise dentistry only in the place for which it was licensed.

§ 2º - The registration of professionals registered in public health agencies until April 14, 1964, can be made regardless of the presentation of the diplomas, upon certificate provided by the competent agencies.

Art. 26 - The Regional Council shall publish, in its bulletin, or in the official body of the territory of its jurisdiction, the list of professionals enrolled in the quarter, and, in separate, the complete list of professionals who are members of its staff, with registration number in the Council.

Art. 27 - To the registered professional, the Council will send a portfolio, according to a single model that is approved by the Federal Council, which will enable it to exercise dentistry.

§ 1 - The professional card of which this article is treated will be valid as an identity document and will have public faith in the form of Article 15 of Law No. 4,324 of April 14, 1964.

§ 2 - In the dentist's medical records will be made notes related to professional activity, including compliments and penalties, at the discretion of the Council.

§ 3- When you stop performing dental activity, the professional will return the portfolio to the Council in which he is enrolled.

Art. 28- After the registration of the professional in the Councils, a stamp will be affixed to the back of the diploma containing the registration data, signed by the President and Secretary of the Council.

Sole Paragraph - In the case of professionals trained by defunct schools or colleges, who do not have diplomas, the above-mentioned stamp will be affixed to the certificates provided by the Ministry of Education and Culture by the Ministry of Health.

Art. 29 - If the dentist enrolled in a Regional Council of Dentistry goes to practice his activities in the region jurisdictioned by another Regional Council, he will be obliged to apply for registration or to apply for a visa in his portfolio.

§ 1 - If it is temporary exercise in another region, thus understood the period of time less than 90 (ninety) days, the Dentist will present his portfolio to be targeted by the President of the Regional Council of the new jurisdiction, who will note the temporary nature of the authorization and the period granted.

§ 2 - If it is an exercise on a permanent basis, leaving the Dentist to perform activities in the region in which he was previously enrolled, he is obliged to request the transfer of his registration to the Council that jurisdiction the new place of their activities.

§ 3º- The permanent and simultaneous dental activity, in the jurisdictions of more than one Regional Council, determines the mandatory registration of the Dentist in each of these Regional Councils, constituting the first in main registration and the others in secondary inscriptions, all noted in the respective professional identity card.

§ 4 - The Regional Council wants to receive application for secondary registration or transfer, may require the interested party to submit all the documents necessary for registration in its framework.

CHAPTER V

PENALTIES

Art. 30- It is up to the Regional Council, in which the dentist was enrolled at the time of the fact punishable, to apply the penalty.

Sole Paragraph - The disciplinary jurisdiction set out in this article does not derogate from the common jurisdiction, where the fact constitutes a misdemeanor or crime provided for by law.

Art. 31- The disciplinary penalties applicable by the Regional Councils to registered dentists are as follows:

a) confidential warning, in reserved notice;
b) confidential censorship, in reserved notice;
c) public censorship, in official publication;
d) suspension of professional practice up to thirty (30) days;
e) Cassation of professional practice, "ad referendum" of the Federal Council.

Sole Paragraph - Except in cases of manifest severity, which require immediate application of a more serious penalty, the imposition of penalties shall comply with the gradation of this article.

CHAPTER VI

OF THE ADMINISTRATIVE PROCESS
FOR INFRACTION TO THE LAW

Art. 32 - Infringement proceedings shall be initiated:
a) by provocation of Counselor;
b) by provocation of union or class association;
c) by complaint of a qualified professional or a third party;
d) by provocation of the Council's tax.

§ 1 - In the event of denunciation, the whistleblower will formulate the same in writing, in two (2) ways, with a firm recognized in the first, pointing out the incriminated facts.

§ 2 - When the accused is A Counselor, the complaint will be processed if the evidential elements of the alleged fact are indicated.

Art. 33 - Received the complaint, the President of the Council, if he deems it necessary, will immediately have the incriminated facts investigated, through his inspection service or, if he considers the infringement proved, will have the respective file drawn up.

Sole Paragraph - The notice of infraction shall be subscribed by one of the Directors of the Board and shall qualify the administrative offense appointed and the penalty appropriate.

Art. 34 - When the incriminated facts involve violation of the Code of Ethics, the notice of infringement will only be drawn up based on the written opinion of the respective committee.

Art. 35 - In the notice of infringement will be given to the infringer the period of 10 (ten) days for defense and proof, which will count from the date of delivery of the copy of the file.

§ 1st - The shipment, when made by mail, will be made with acknowledgement of receipt.

§ 2 - When the infringer refuses to receive the copy of the notice of infringement or obstruct scans, the proceedings will proceed, making the refusal or obstruction appear in it.

§ 3 - In the event that the offender is not found, the process will run by default, being designated by the President of the Council, Defensor Dativo.

§ 4 - The dative defender may not be an Effective Or Alternate Councillor.

Art. 36. After the defense is presented, the process will be distributed to a Counselor to report the achievement.

Single paragraph. Before delivering his opinion, which should be conclusive, the rapporteur may determine that further evidence be submitted or request clarification on the issue of law.

Art. 37 - The trial may be converted into due diligence, to elucidate facts or a question of law.

Art. 38 - The outcome of the trial must be communicated to the infringer in writing, granting him a period of 30 (thirty) days to appeal.

§ 1º - When a penalty of fine is imposed, the appeal will only continue if the applicant deposits the respective value within the period of the appeal.

§ 2 - The appeal will have suspensive effect only when the decision commins penalty of suspension or cassation of professional practice.

§ 3 - The appeal will be forwarded to the Federal Council accompanied by the entire infringement and information process of the Regional Council.

Article 39 - The Federal Council will consider the appeal after it has been reported by one of its Directors.

Sole Paragraph - The decision of the Federal Council shall not be appealed, except that it involves impeachment of the term of Office of A Director.

Art. 40- Given the decision, the case shall be lowered to the Regional Council for the execution of the judgment.

Art. 41 - The appeal is unfounded, in the event of a fine, the deposit will be appropriated as payment.

Art. 42 - In the event of suspension or impeachment of the professional practice, the Regional Council shall notify the interested party in writing, for collection of the Professional Card, and communicate the fact to the health authority of the region and to the competent public agencies, when the infringer exercises public function.

Article 43 - In the event of impeachment of the Term of Office of the Director, it will be up to review appeal, with suspensive effect, to be brought within 15 (fifteen) days, addressed to the Federal Council itself.

Art. 44 - The interested party may follow the infringement process, in person, or through a legally constituted attorney.

CHAPTER VII

OF JUDICIAL COLLECTION
OF ACTIVE DEBT

Art. 45 - The judicial collection of the active debt of the Federal and Regional Councils of Dentistry will be made by the fiscal executive process, regulated in Decree-Law No. 960 of December 17, 1938 and subsequent legislation.

Sole Paragraph - Active debt is understood arising from fees, fines, annuities, contributions and fees.

Art. 46 - If the amicable payment of the active debt is not made, the Regional Council will register it in the relevant book in it, making it appear:

I- its origin and nature;
II - the amount due;
III - the name of the debtor and, where possible, his domicile and address.

Art. 47 - To begin the process, the certificate of the active debt will be extracted, proceeding to judicial collection.

CHAPTER VIII

ELECTIONS

Art. 48 - The effective and alternate members of the Federal Council of Dentistry shall be elected by the Delegates-Electors of the Regional Councils in a ballot that must be held at least 30 (thirty) days before the end of the term of office of the Directors in office.

§ 1º- It is ineligible for the function of Delegate-Elector and his alternate the Dentist who presides over the Assembly in which they are elected.

§ 2nd - The Assembly of Delegates-Voters will be convened by the President of the Federal Council, through publication in the "Official Gazette" of the Union and personal correspondence, addressed to delegates-voters, at least 30 (thirty) days before the date set for its realization.

§ 3- The date of the election, fixed by the Federal Council, will be announced in the "Official Gazette" of the Union at least 120 (one hundred and twenty) days before its completion.

§ 4º- Up to 60 (sixty) days before the date fixed for the election will be received at the Secretariat of the Federal Council the registration of plates, each containing 9 (nine) names of candidates for effective members and equal number of candidates for alternates, accompanied by the "*curriculum vitae*" of each candidate.

§ 5º- Dentists of Brazilian nationality, registered in the Regional Council, who have not suffered penalties, do not have geographical restriction to professional practice, and are not Delegates-Electors may be included in the plates.

§ 6- The President of the Federal Council shall declare the plate presented:

(a) by 20 (twenty) dentists, or

b) by 5 (five) presidents of the Regional Council.

§ 7º - Each signatory can only subscribe to the application for registration of a plate.

§ 8 - The plates will be numbered according to the order of entry of the respective requirements in the Secretariat of the Federal Council.

§ 9th - Up to 50 (fifty) days before the date set for the election, the Federal Council will forward to all Regional Councils the list of the plates registered, with the names of the respective applicants and the "curriculum vitae" of each candidate.

§ 10 - The challenges to any name or plate may be made in writing and justifiably up to 30 (thirty) days before the date fixed for the election, and must be immediately assessed by the Board of Directors of the Federal Council.

§ 11 - Once the appeal has been verified, the Federal Council shall notify its signatories, giving them a period of 10 (ten) days for the replacement of the name or plate challenged.

§ 12th - Once the absolute majority of the voters for one of the plates is verified, the President of the Assembly will proclaim the result of the election and will draw up the respective minutes, which will be signed by the President and all delegates-voters.

§ 13 - If the legal quorum is not reached, the second election will be held immediately, the latter running only the two most voted plates.

Art. 49 - The effective and alternate members of the Regional Councils shall be elected by an absolute majority of votes of dentists enrolled in their board, in an election that must be held at least 60 (sixty) days before the end of the term of office of the Directors in office.

§ 1st- Candidates must organize plates containing 5 (five) names for full members and 5 (five) for alternates.

§ 2nd - The plates will be entered at the request of at least 10 (ten) registered dentists, even with the Treasury and in full enjoyment of their professional rights. Registration must precede 30 (thirty) days the date scheduled for the election, and there may be challenges of names or plate entered within 72 (seventy-two) hours, provided it is reasoned and subscribed by 10 (ten) or more Dentists.

§ 3- The challenge of candidate or plate can only be decreed by a vote of 4/5 (four fifths) of the members of the Regional Council.

§ 4 - If recognized by the Regional Council, the challenge, the plate reached will have the period of 3 (three) days to replace the name or the contested names.

Art. 50- The election will be announced in the official body of the State, the Territory or the Federal District, and in a newspaper of great circulation, 30 (thirty) days in advance.

§ 1st - The vote is mandatory and personal in each election, except absence due to illness or force major, fully proven, within 8 (eight) days of the election.

§ 2nd - Due to unjustified lack of election will incur the Dentist in a fine of 5% (five percent) of the highest minimum wage in force in the country, paid double in recidivism.

§ 3º- The Dentist who is absent from his electoral zone may vote by mail, in double letter, opaque, closed, sent to the President of the Regional Council, through a letter with a recognized firm, and posted under registration in the Post office and Telegraph.

§ 4- The ballots received, with the formalities of the previous paragraph, will be computed until the end of the vote. The larger overcard will be opened by the President of the Council, who will deposit the minor overcarta at the ballot box, without violating the secrecy of the vote.

§ 5th- In each election, votes will be received for at least 6 (six) consecutive hours.

Art. 51 - The election to the Regional Council will be made by secret ballot, at the council's office, and there may be other places to receive the votes, when the number of voters exceeds 200 (two hundred), in this case, each place, 3 (three) professionals designated by the Council.

§ 1°- The Regional Council may divide the territory of its jurisdiction into electoral zones, for the purpose of installing polling stations, so that each has at least 200 (professionals) in a position to vote, designating for each zone an electoral board composed of 3 (three) members.

§ 2 - After the end of the vote, the President of each receiving table will have minutes drawn up of the papers, in which the number of votes taken and the occurrences will be declared.

§ 3- The minutes of the work, the ballot box and the voting sheets shall be sent through one of the members of the bureau to the council's office, in sealed casing, which will carry the signatures of the pollsors and the inspectors.

§ 4° - The electoral area of which the 1st is treated may cover several neighboring municipalities, and the components of the electoral board should be chosen preferably among the representatives of the Council in the region.§

§ 5 - To vote, the voter identifies himself before the table, signs the voting list, receives the single ballot on which the competing plates are registered, identified by order number of the application for registration; he goes to the cabin, folds the ballot and deposits it in the urn.

Article 52 - The President of the Council, received at the ballot box, shall determine, within a maximum period of five (5) days, its calculation.

§ 1 - The postal vote will only be determined if received until the end of the vote.

§ 2nd - After the calculation, the President of the Council will declare elected the plate that obtains an absolute majority of the votes of registered Dentists and will report the result to the Federal Council of Dentistry, for proclamation.

§ 3- If the absolute majority is not obtained, the election will be repeated within 20 (twenty) days, with the two most voted plates, considering elected to which it obtains an absolute majority of voters.

§ 4°- Persisting the lack of number, the President of the Federal Council of Dentistry, after hearing the Plenary, will appoint Dentists, to integrate, on a provisional basis, the Regional Council, in accordance with point "e", article 4 of Law No. 4,324, of April 14, 1964.

Art. 53 - If there is no reasoned appeal within 72 (seventy-two) hours, the Federal Council of Dentistry will proclaim the result of the election.

Art. 54- Proclaimed the result of the election, the new members of the Regional Council will be sworn in by the President whose term of office is extinguished.

CHAPTER IX

GENERAL PROVISIONS

Art. 55 - The Federal Council may intervene in the Regional Councils, appointing provisional Board to clean up irregularities and promote elections, in one of the following hypotheses:

a) manifest inoperability of the Regional Council;

b) non-compliance by the Council with legal rules or resolutions of the Federal Council.

§ 1 - The act of intervention, which will matter in the dismissal of the members in office of the Regional Council, will be preceded by summary investigation by special delegate and will only be enacted by the vote of 2/3 (two thirds) of the Federal Council.

§ 2- The provisional Board shall have a maximum period of 180 (one hundred and eighty) days to rescan the irregularities and call the election of the new members of the Regional Council, with the provisional board of directors being allowed to participate in the competing plates.

§ 3º- Fulfilled its mission, the Provisional Board will report its activities to the Federal Council, including the result of the election and request for proclamation of the elected.

Article 56 - In the deadlines that are established in resolution, the Regional Councils will send to the Federal Council the annual budget proposal and the accountability, as well as the statement of revenue collected, accompanied by the quota due to the Federal Council.

Article 57 - The Federal Council and the Regional Councils of Dentistry are subject to the standards established in the Federal Public Accounting Code and complementary legislation.

Art. 58 - The Federal Council and the Regional Councils of Dentistry may institute a journal for the dissemination of their activities.

Art. 59 - The staff at the service of the Federal Council and the Regional Councils of Dentistry is governed by labor legislation and registered with the National Institute of Social Security.

Art, i'm sorry. 60- The Federal Council of Dentistry shall take action with the competent bodies to be transferred to it amount equal to 40% (forty percent) of the entire union contribution paid by dentists in 1964, in the form of Article 26 of Law No. 4,324, of April 14, 1964, and 20% (twenty percent) of the entire union contribution paid by the same professionals in subsequent years, in the form of Art. 8(a) of that Law.

Art. 61- As long as the Federal Council of Dentistry is not prepared and approved, the Code of Dental Ethics, after hearing the Regional Councils, will be in force, with the caveat of article 16, the "The Code of Professional Ethics of the Brazilian Dental Union" , approved by the National Deliberative Council of the Brazilian Dental Union, current Brazilian Dental Association, at the VI Brazilian Dental Congress.

Art. 62 - According to Law No. 4,324, of April 14, 1964, the Executive Branch will take measures for the decent installation of regional councils in the Federal District and in the Capitals of the States and Territories, as much as possible in public buildings.

Art. 63 - The Federal Council of Dentistry will lower the resolutions that are deemed necessary for the full functioning of the Regional Councils, complementing this Regulation.

Art. 64- Banco do Brasil S.A. will transfer to the account of the Federal Council of Dentistry the share of 20% (twenty percent) of the union contribution paid by dentists throughout Brazil, regardless of authorization of the unions concerned.

Art. 65 - This Decree will enter into force on the date of its publication, repealing the provisions to the contrary.

Brasilia, July 3, 1971;

150th of Independence and 83rd of the Republic.

EMÍLIO G. MEDICI

José Flávio Pécora
Jargas G. Passarinho
Júlio Barata

F - CFO Resolution - 179/91 - Dental Ética Code

Code of Dental Ethics (APPROVED BY RESOLUTION CFO-179, OF DECEMBER 19, 1991)(Amended by Regulation No. 01, 05.06.98)The text was based on the Final Report of the 1st NATIONAL CONFERENCE ON DENTAL ETHICS - I CONEO, held in Vitória(ES), by the Federal Council and Regional Councils of Dentistry, in 1991.Resolution CFO - 179/91 Repeals the Code of Dental Ethics approved by Resolution CFO-151, july 16, 1983 and approves another in place. The President of the Federal Council of Dentistry, in the exercise of his regimental duties, fulfilling the deliberation of the Plenary, in an extraordinary meeting, held on this date, RESOLVE: Art. 1. The Code of Dental Ethics, approved by resolution CFO/151 of July 16, 1983.Art. 2, is repealed. The Code of Dental Ethics is approved, which is publica.Art. 3. This Resolution enters into force on 1 January 1992. Rio de Janeiro, December 19, 1991.ORLANDO LIMONGI, CD JOÃO HILDO DE CARVALHO FURTADO, CD GENERAL SECRETARY PRESIDENT

CHAPTER IPRELIMINARYPROVISIONSArt. First. Code of Dental Ethics regulates the rights and duties of professionals and entities with registration in the Dentistry Councils, according to their específicas.Art. 2. Dentistry is a profession that is practiced, for the benefit of the health of the human being and the collectivity, without discrimination in any form or pretext. CHAPTER IIDOS FUNDAMENTAL RIGHTSArt. Third. They constitute fundamental rights of the enrolled professionals, according to their specific attributions:I - to diagnose, plan and execute treatments, with freedom of conviction, within the limits of their attributions, observed the current state of science and its professional dignity;

II - safeguard professional secrecy;III - contract professional services in accordance with the precepts of this Code;IV - refuse to practice the profession in public or private sphere where working conditions are not dignified, safe and healthy.

CHAPTER IIIOF FUNDAMENTAL DUTIESART. 4th. They are fundamental duties of the registered professionals:I - to exercise the profession maintaining dignified behavior;II - to keep up to date the professional

and cultural knowledge necessary for the full performance of professional practice;III - to ensure the health and dignity of the patient;IV - to keep professional secrecy; V - promote collective health in the performance of their functions, positions and citizenship, regardless of whether they practice the profession in the public or private sector;VI - prepare the clinical records of patients, keeping them in their own file; VII - to point out flaws in the regulations and norms of the institutions in which they work, when it deems them unworthy for the practice of the profession or harmful to the patient, and should address, in such cases, the competent bodies; VII - to point out flaws in the regulations and norms of the institutions in which they work, when it deems them unworthy for the practice of the profession or harmful to the patient, and should address in such cases, to the competent bodies; VIII - advocate for harmony in class; IX - to refrain from the practice of acts that imply the commodification of dentistry or its misconceptualization; X - take responsibility for the acts performed; XI - safeguard patient privacy throughout the service.

Chapter V DO RELATIONSHIP Section I With Patient Art. 6th. It constitutes an ethical infraction: I - exaggerating in diagnosis, prognosis or therapy; II - fail to adequately clarify the purposes, risks, costs and alternatives of treatment; III - to perform or propose unnecessary treatment or for which it is not qualified; IV - abandon patient, except for justifiable reasons, circumstance in which the fees and indicated substitute will be reconciled; V - fail to attend a patient seeking professional care in case of emergency, when there is no other dentist in a position to do so; VI - initiate treatment of minors without authorization of their guardians or legal representatives, except in cases of urgency or emergency; VII - disrespect or allow the patient to be disrespected; VIII - adopt new techniques or materials that do not have effective scientific evidence; IX - provide a certificate that does not correspond to the veracity of the coded facts (cid) or those that have not participated. Section II With the Health Team: Art. 7. In the relationship between the members of the health team, respect, loyalty and collaboration will be maintained técnico-científica. Art. 8. It constitutes an ethical offence: I - diverting customer from colleague;

II - assume employment or function succeeding the professional dismissed or removed in reprisal for the attitude of defense of legitimate movement of the category or application of this code; III - to practice or allow unfair competition to be practiced; IV - be conniving in technical errors or ethical infractions; V - unjustifiably deny emergency technical collaboration or professional services to colleagues; VI - criticize technical-scientific error of absent colleague, except through representation to the Regional Council; VII - exploit colleague in employment relationships or when sharing fees; VIII - to assign office or laboratory, without compliance with the relevant legislation; IX - use of services provided by professionals not legally qualified.

Chapter VI DO PROFESSIONAL SECRECY Art. 9th. It constitutes an ethical offense: I - to reveal, without just cause, a confidential fact that you are aware of because of the exercise of his profession; II - neglect in the guidance of its employees regarding professional secrecy. § 1. It is understood as a just cause, mainly: a) compulsory notification of illness; b) collaboration with justice in cases provided for by law; c) dental expertise within its exact limits; d) strict defense of legitimate interest of registered professionals; e) disclosure of a confidential fact to the person responsible for the incapacitated. § 2º. It does not constitute a breach of professional secrecy the decline of the treatment undertaken, in the judicial collection of professional fees.

Chapter VIII
OF THE SPECIALTIES Art. 12th. The exercise and announcement of the specialties in Dentistry shall comply with the provisions of this Chapter and the rules of the Federal. Art. 13th. The specialist, attending patient forwards by dentist, will act only in the area of his specialty. Sole Paragraph. After care, the patient will be returned with the pertinentes. Art. 14. It is vetoed to call itself an expert without registration in the Regional. Art. 15th. For diagnostic and treatment purposes, the specialist may confer with other professionals. Chapter IX DA HOSPITAL DENTISTRy Art. 16th. It is the dentist's responsibility to hospitalize and assist patients in public and private hospitals, with and without philanthropic character, respecting the technical and administrative standards of institutions. Art. 17th.

Dental activities carried out in hospital shall comply with the rules of the Federal.Art. 18th. It constitutes an ethical infraction, even in a hospital environment, to perform surgical intervention outside the scope of Dentistry.Chapter XDAS ENTITIES PROVIDING ORALHEALTH CARE. 19th. Clinics, cooperatives, companies and other dental service providers and/or contractors apply to the provisions of this Chapter and those of the Federal Council.

Art. 20. The registered professionals, when owners, or the technical responsible will respond jointly and severally with the offender for ethical infractions cometidas.Art. 21. The entities mentioned in Article 19 are obliged to:I - maintain the technical-scientific quality of the work carried out; II - provide the professional with minimum facilities conditions, material resources

, human and technological conditions defined by the Federal Council of Dentistry, which ensure their full and safe performance, except in conditions of emergency or imminent danger of life;III - maintain constant dental audits, through trained professionals;IV - be restricted to the preparation of oral health plans or programs that have technical, administrative and financial support; V - keep users informed about the features available for atendê-los.Art. 22° . It constitutes an ethical infraction:I - to proclaim unrealistic advantages in order to establish competition with similar entities; II - offer treatment below the recommended quality standards. III - execute and advertise free work for the purpose of grooming;IV - announce specialties without the respective registrations of experts in the Regional Council; V - to use the economic power in order to establish competition with similar entities or professionals individually;VI - to propose remuneration for the services provided by professionals linked to it on bases lower than the National Table of Agreements and Accreditations.VIII - not to keep users informed about the resources available for the service and fail to respond to their complaints. Chapter XIIDAS ENTITIES OF CLASSEArt. Twenty-five. It is up to the entities of the class, through its president, to make the relevant communications that are of indisputable public interest. Single paragraph. This assignment may be delegated, without prejudice to the joint and several liability of titular.Art. 26. The president and the offender are responsible for ethical infractions committed on behalf of entidade.Art. 27. It constitutes an ethical infraction:I - to use the entity for its own promotion or personal advantages; II - harm morally or materially the entity; III - use the name of the entity to promote commercial products without them having been tested and proven their effectiveness in the form of the Law; IV - disrespect entity, revile or defame its directors. Chapter XIII (*)

COMMUNICATIONArt. Twenty-eightth. The communication in Dentistry will comply with the provisions of this Chapter and the specifications of the Regional Councils, approved by the Federal Council.

Section lOf Advertising, Advertising and AdvertisingArt. Twenty-nine. Advertisements, advertising and advertising may be made through the media, following the precepts of this Code and the veracity, decency, respectability and honestidade.Art. 30. In the advertisements, signs and printed should appear:- the name of the professional;- the profession;- the number of registration in the Regional Council.Single paragraph. It may also include :I - the specialties in which the dentist is enrolled;II - the titles of academic training "stricto sensu" and the teaching profession;III - address, telephone, fax, e-mail address, working hours, agreements and accreditations;IV - facilities, equipment and treatment techniques; V - logo and/or logo;VI - the expression "GENERAL PRACTITIONER", by professionals who perform activities relevant to dentistry arising from knowledge acquired in the course of graduação.Art. 31°. It constitutes an ethical infringement: I - announcing prices and payment modality; II - announcing securities that it does not have; III - advertising techniques and/or treatments that have no scientific proof; IV - criticize techniques used by other professionals as being inadequate or outdated; V - to consult, diagnose or prescribe treatment through any mass communication vehicle, as well as to allow their participation in the dissemination of dental matters to cease to have an exclusive character of clarification and education of the community; VI - disclose name, address or any other element that identifies the patient, unless with his free and informed consent, or its legal guardian; VII - enticing patients; VIII - to induce public opinion to believe that there is a reserve of clinical action for certain procedures; IX - to announce dental specialty not regulated by the Federal Council of Dentistry; X - to disclose or allow public observations about the clinical performance or any manifestation related to the performance of another professional.

Art. 32. Companies that explore the various branches of dentistry, such as clinics, cooperatives, health care plans, insurance, accreditations, administrators, intermediaries, health insurers and congeners, apply the rules of this Chapter.

Chapter XIV OF SCIENTIFIC RESEARCH Art. Thirty-five. It constitutes an ethical violation: I - failure to comply with the rules of the competent body and the legislation on health research; II - to use experimental animals without clear and honest objectives to enrich the horizons of dental knowledge and, consequently, to expand the benefits to society; III - disrespect the legal limitations of the profession in cases of experience in anima nobili; IV - to violate the legislation regulating the use of the cadaver for the study and/or exercises of surgical techniques; V - to break the legislation regulating transplants of organs and tissues post-mortem and the "living body itself"; VI - conduct research on a human being without this or its guardian, or legal representative, having given written consent after being duly informed about the nature and consequences of the research; VII - use, experimentally without authorization from the competent authority, and without the prior knowledge and consent of the patient or his legal representative, any type of therapy not yet released for use in the country.

Chapter XV

OF THE FEATHERS AND THEIR APPLICATIONS

Art. 36. The precepts of this Code are mandatory and its violation will subject the infringer and who, in any case, with him to compete for the infringement, the following penalties provided for in Article 17 of the Statute of 10 July 1998:

I - reserved warning;

II - public censorship;

III - suspension of professional practice, up to one hundred and eighty (180) days, "ad referendum" of the Federal Council; IV - impeachment of the professional practice "ad referendum" of the Federal._____ (*) Drafting given by the

Statute approved in 10.07.98.Art. 37. Except in cases of manifest severity and requiring immediate application of a more serious penalty, the imposition of penalties will comply with the gradation of the previous article.

Sole Paragraph. Severity is evaluated by the extent of the damage and its conseqüências.Art. 38º. It is considered of manifest gravity, mainly:

I - impute to someone an unethical fact that he knows him innocent, causing the establishment of an ethical process; II - cover up or give evidence to the illegal exercise of the profession;III - to exercise, after being alerted, dental activity in an illegal, inidônea or irregular entity;IV - occupy a position whose professional has been removed from it due to a class movement; V - exercise a private act of a dentist, without being legally qualified for this; VI - maintain professional activity during the term of suspensive penalty; VII - practice or engage activity torpe.Art. 39º. The claim of ignorance or poor understanding of the precepts of this Code does not exclude the penalty infrator.Art. 40. These are circumstances that may mitigate the penalty:I - not having been convicted before of ethical offense;II - have repaired or mitigated the dano.Art. 41st. Cumulatively, the amount of the annum in force may be applied to the infringer, which will vary from one to fifty times, and may also be converted into free community service at the request of the apenado.

(*) Wording given by the Statute approved on 10.07.98.Chapter XVIFINALPROVISIONSArt. 42nd. The professional convicted of ethical offense to the penalties provided for in Article 36 of this Code, may be subject to rehabilitation, in the manner provided for in the Code of Ethical Odontológico.Art. 43rd. The amendments to this Code are the exclusive competence of the Federal Council, after hearing the Regionais.Art. Forty-four. This Code will enter into force on January 1, 1992.

G - Jurisprudence

Dental and anesthetic error will support monthly pension of almost R$ 7,000.

Almost nine years after the ill-fated dental surgery that resulted in a vegetative state of the minor Francis Aguiar, the dentist Irani Zanettini and the anesthesiologist Vilmar

Molon were heavily convicted in civil action, which has been pending since July 1997. The sentence is the judge Viviane Miranda Becker, the 3rd Civil Court of Caxias do Sul. The doctor and dentist will have to pay a lifetime pension of 37.95 monthly minimum wages (R$ 6,831.00). Since July 1997, the two professionals have been paying 24 minimum wages (R$ 4,320.00), to pay for part of Francis' treatment. They have also been expected to pay alimony of a minimum wage since January 14, 1993, when Francis underwent the procedure and never left the vegetative state. The cost of treatment varies between R$ 5,000 and R$ 6,000 per month, including medications, maintenance of nurses, diapers and physiotherapy.

The dentist and anesthesiologist will still have to pay R $ 130 thousand, corrected, since the date of the fact. This amount, according to Solon Francis' father, refers to what was spent by the family in the first four years of treatment. *"We had to sell real estate and ask for money for relatives,"* he recalls, speaking to The Pioneer newspaper. The compensation for moral damages was stipulated in 800 minimum wages – 400 for the young and 400 for the parents. It will be up to the dentist to pay 40% and, to the doctor, bear 60% of the value. The parties may still use the TJRS.

JUDICIARY
PARANAVAÍ DISTRICT - 1ST CRIMINAL COURT

Seen and examined these criminal case files, registered under no. 23/97, in which the Ministry of Public and defendant Fulano

I - REPORT

The Public Prosecutor's Office agent with attributions in this Region offered a complaint against Fulano, a Brazilian single dentist (CRO/SP no. X X X, born in SP, at X X X, son of PAI and MÃE, resident in this city, in RUA X X X X, next to the no. X X X X, by the practice of the following criminal fact:

"On June 3, 1995, from 5:00 p.m. to 7:00 p.m., in the office of the accused, located on XXXXXXX Street, next to the number X X X, the dentist Fulano, culpable acting with manifest recklessness, neglecting the basic duties of his profession, art and craft, when subjecting the victim [Cicrano] to a dental procedure consistent in the extraction of a tooth (third molar), fractured the tooth and left it without extracting, causing the offending of the body lesions of a mild nature, described in the dental diagnosis of fls. 17 – "there was an attempt to surgically extract the left lower third molar by another dentist, in addition to presenting left lower lip paraesthesia with hematoma and edema (...) then, the infected site was x-rayed, and after radiographic examination, 60% of the third molar fractured and impacted and loss of the total lingual bone table (...) being performed in the sequence the partial suture of skin because there was tissue destruction in an attempt to remove with another surgeon" and report of body lesions of fls. 18, verse (iatrogenic lesion - dental error)."
1st

In doing so, the accused would have incurred in the penalties of Article 129, §§ 6, and 7 of the Penal Code.

After the complaint was received, the defendant was regularly cited by mandate but did not attend the designated interrogation. As a result, his default was decreed, with the consequent appointment who then presented the previous defense.

In the course of the procedural investigation, four prosecution witnesses were heard, the same as those filed by the defense.

After the phase of Article 499 of the Code of Criminal Procedure, the parties presented their final submissions. The ministerial agent postulated the conviction of the defendant for the practice of the crime provided for in § 6 of Article 129 of the Penal Code, without the incidence of the increase in the penalty provided for in § 7 of that legal article [5].

The defense, in turn, advocated for the acquittal of the defendant, with the fulcrum in the thesis that there was no malpractice on the part of the defendant because the tooth was already inflamed at its root and that it was a complicated extraction. He maintained that he was arranged with the victim of this return the next day to finish the extraction, but he did not return to the office.

II - RATIONALIZATION

In the case in question, the victim attended the defendant's office, complaining of pain in a tooth (third molar). After examining the patient, the defendant decided to subject him to a dental procedure for tooth extraction. However, the surgery failed because the defendant could not extract the tooth in its entirety, and the world left this fractured, thus causing minor bodily injuries to the patient.

Therefore, according to the initial accusatory piece, the defendant would have acted with manifest recklessness, neglecting the essential duties of his profession, art, and craft.

Despiciendo says that negligence is the opposite of diligence, which comes from the Latin word diligere – act with love, care, and attention, avoiding any distractions and failures. Therefore, based diligence is always an omission of the recommended behaviors derived from the shared experience or the particular requirements of medical practice.

On the other hand, Malpractice is the lack of observation of norms, lack of technical knowledge of the profession, and practical unpreparedness. Malpractice also characterizes the inability to exercise a certain office due to lack of skill or lack of the necessary, rudimentary knowledge required in a profession.

On the basis of these considerations and analyzing the evidence carried out in the file, it can be <u>perfectly concluded that the defendant was negligent and unexpert in his action, for the following reasons:</u>

First, because the defendant did not subject the patient to an X-ray to analyze the state of the tooth. This is a basic procedure before any extraction. Now, if the defendant knew of the need for radiography but did not perform it, he was negligent in his behavior. If he did not know that radiography was necessary, it is clear that he was imperitoly unexpert, because he did not have the necessary knowledge to practice his profession.

Malpractice, on the other hand, is the lack of observation of norms, lack of technical knowledge of the profession, practical unpreparedness. Malpractice also characterizes the inability to exercise a certain office due to a lack of skill or absence of the necessary, rudimentary knowledge required in a profession.

Based on these considerations and analyzing the evidence carried out in the file, it can be <u>perfectly concluded that the defendant was negligent and unexpert in his action for the following reasons:</u>

First, because the defendant did not subject the patient to an X-ray to analyze the state of the tooth, this is a basic procedure before any extraction. Second, if the defendant knew of the need for radiography but did not perform it, he was negligent in his behavior. Third, if he did not realize that radiography was necessary, it is clear that he was imperiously unexpert because he did not have the knowledge needed to practice his profession.

Considering the injuries produced on the victim and taking into account his degree of distaste in view of the de facto situation in which his conduct occurred, **culpability** should be considered to a high degree; who has a good **record**; that their social **conduct** is normal; that his **personality** is not focused on crime, for it was a

Isolated act in his life; that there is **no motive** for the crime; whereas **the victim's** behavior did not contribute to the defendant's attitude; that the **consequences of the crime were** severe because the victim suffered a lot of pain and had to bear enormous expenses for the performance of another surgery and treatment of the fractured tooth; fixed to him the **basic penalty at its legal minimum, that is, in a year of detention, this penalty that becomes definitive, in the absence of extenuating or aggravating circumstances and special causes of increase or decreases.**

I set the open regime for the beginning of the execution of the sentence (Penal Code, art. 33, § 3) by complying with the following conditions:

a) during the entire penalty period, must provide services to the community, in the form of donation of a monthly basic basket to the Municipal Public Jail, in the individual amount of R$ 50.00 (fifty reais). The basic baskets must be delivered to the Registry of this Criminal Court, and the Registrar will be responsible for referring them to the Public Jail;

1. Must retire to his residence in the period between 20:00 and 06:00 hours and on weekends and holidays and appear in person in Court to inform and justify his activities. In addition, he will not be able to leave the district where he resides, for more than ten days, without the authorization of the Court.

I also order the defendant to pay the costs and costs of proceedings.

After the transit in court, throw the defendant's name on the list of the guilty.

Officiate to, the Regional Council of Dentistry of São Paulo, scientific sign the present condemnation for adopting the appropriate measures, including sending certified photocopies of this sentence.

In compliance, the provisions contained in the Code of Rules of the General Internal Affairs of Justice shall be fulfilled.

Public-it.

Register-it.

Intimate, the defendant, personally or by mandate, if not found, and his defender, in addition to the representative of the public prosecutor.

Paranavaí, October 6, 1998.

Álvaro Rodrigues Junior
Judge of Law

- Civil liability of the dentist for the manufacture of dental prosthesis:

Dental prosthesis - Conclusive expert evidence - demonstrated the incursion of treatment regarding the lower right arch - Duty to indemnify - Impossibility of analysis of the rest of the work performed - Replacement of the prosthesis by another professional - Correct sentence - Resources devoid.
Judgment No 2047 - 6th Civil Chamber
Ap. Civil - 0061394-9.

- Civil liability for root canal trepanation:

Civil liability - Dentist - Unsatisfactory execution of the services, obliging the author to redo them, as well as to pay them again to another professional - Condemnation of the defendant in the return of the amount received - Embargoes rejected.
Injunctred infringing no. 183.274-2 - São Paulo - Embargante: Wilson Mestriner - Injuncted : José Roberto Santucci.

- Dentist's civil liability for aesthetic damage:

Civil liability - Dentist - No causal link between the author's complaints and the surgical intervention performed therein - Conduct of the professional supported by the experts and the specialized literature - Budget not due - Resource not provided.
Civil Appeal no. 13.985-4 - São Paulo – Appeal: Marlene Aparecida Sanchez - Appealed: José Arnaldo Braghetti. (JTJ - Volume 182 - Page 94).

H - Cases of Dental Errors Abroad

Jan-01-01, 07:46 PM (CST) "nerve damage from bone graft surgery"[122]

I had surgery. My dentist, an implantology specialist, suggested that I needed surgery to regenerate bone; he used synthetic materials. He mentioned that I needed this

---

[122] Nerve injury resulting from bone graft surgery. (our translation). http://www.sciential.net/cgi-bin/dcforum/dcboard.cgi?az=view_ip&forum=DCForumID5&om=13&omm=0&name=Cecilie%20%28Guest%29. Access on 01/01/2001.

surgery for the implants that needed to be placed in the lower-left area of my mouth. All in all, the surgery lasted 2 1/2 hours. I was so leary going into it. Although I trusted my dentist. I had a terrible suspicion that said don't do it. I now wish I would have followed that premonition and not had anything done. This Wednesday, it's going on 4 weeks, and I can't feel half of my lower lip, and the numbness extends to my chin. I called my dentist, and he said that I needed time and that some patients take up to four months. He also mentioned that this could be permanent. He sounded so discouraging to me. My surgery was different from the ones I had read about on this site. Most injuries are due to injections. Is there anyone out there that has had this type of surgery? Since I have complete numbness on half of my lower lip and chin, does that mean I probably won't regain any feeling? Please, if there is anyone out there who has undergone this type of surgery and has had the problems I am having, please answer! December 6th, 2000

DENTISTS KEEP A CAUTIOUS EYE ON IOM RECOMMENDATIONS

CHICAGO (November 17, 2000)-Dentists have expressed concern that a mandatory medical error reporting system proposed by the Institute of Medicine (IOM) report, To Err is Human, could lead to confidentiality problems and increased litigation.

While the report focuses on medicine-mostly in hospitals-it is clear that a central database of medical errors would also affect dentistry.

Dentists hold that the types of mistakes discussed in the report are rare in dentistry. Moreover, while there are isolated injury incidents due to dentist error, few dental office mishaps result in death or severe harm.

"Not to say that mistakes don't happen, but the consequences are not nearly as severe as in medicine," says Vincent C. Mayher, Jr., DMD, FAGD, Academy trustee, and former member of the Academy's Council on Legislative and Governmental Affairs.

Under the proposal for mandatory reporting, hospitals (and eventually all places where patients receive care) would be responsible for reporting such events to state governments. Currently, about a third of the states have their own mandatory reporting requirements, according to the U.S. Department of Health and Human Services (HHS).

For dentists, talk of reporting systems raises the specter of the National Practitioner Data Bank, which has been tweaking health care providers' nerves ever since its inception in 1986 by the Bureau of Health Professions, Health Resources and Services Administration of the HHS. The Data Bank, designed to collect information on unprofessional behavior, malpractice payments, and disciplinary action and other licensure information by state boards, has been in the news recently as a number of forces push to open its records to the public.

Myron Bromberg, DDS, chair of the Academy's Council on Legislative and Governmental Affairs, says he has serious concerns about any plans for new reporting systems. Dentists were given repeated promises that the information contained within the Data Bank would never become public. "Yet here we are," he says, "facing Congressional pressure to open it to the public."

The new reporting system will be redundant and open doctors up to even greater risk of damaging information being released to patients, says Dr. Mayher.

Critics are not comforted by promises of confidentiality and safeguards in an era when most people have access and the ability to post information on the World Wide Web. "I don't see why we need another reporting system," said Dr. Mayher. "As far as I can see, this will just be Data Bank Two."

The Academy of General Dentistry is a non-profit organization of more than 37,000 general dentists dedicated to staying up-to-date in the profession through continuing education. A general dentist is the primary care provider for patients of all ages and is responsible for the diagnosis, treatment, management and overall coordination of services related to patient's oral health needs.

The Redwoods Group Dentists Insurance Program

QUICK NEWS

Children Are Dying in the Dentist Chair

By: JULIE SEVRENS
The Salt Lake Tribune
Thursday, June 1, 2000

Jonathan Hess went to a dentist to have a few teeth pulled and came back with severe brain damage.

Javier Villa and Torrie Price never did come home again.

The boys, all younger than 9 and all undergoing routine dental procedures, were felled by sedatives meant to calm them. And each was a victim of dental providers who allegedly underestimated the power of the drugs.

A disturbing trend is emerging across the nation: Oral-sedation deaths -- once unheard of -- are being reported more and more.

It isn't that the drugs themselves are thought to be unsafe. Since the most common sedative, chloral hydrate, was introduced in 1869, it has been used on millions of patients without problem, says Peter Hartmann, past president of the California Board of Dental Examiners.

Adverse consequences, he says, usually can be attributed to human error -- dentist error.

In fact, in the handful of oral-sedation mortality cases in California during the past decade, there has been a tragic pattern of gross negligence on the part of the dentists, Hartmann says. Usually, the dentist has overdosed the patient and then failed to realize something was going wrong because he or she was not monitoring a patient's vital signs

"These aren't accidents," says Hartmann. "These are tragedies."

And the number of tragedies has been steadily growing every year

While there were few known events before the 1990s, nationwide, more than 95 cases involving children and oversedation have now been identified. The majority -- 51 -- ended in death. And researchers at Northwestern University, who reviewed adverse incidents stemming from sedatives, found at least nine children have suffered permanent neurological injuries.

Although children are sedated in several medical settings, a disproportionate number of the incidents occurred in dental offices.

"This is just the tip of the iceberg. I suspect there were many, many more [cases] than we were

able to find," says Charles J. Cote, professor of anesthesiology and pediatrics at the university, whose research was published in April

But many dental experts emphasize that such incidents are still rare and isolated.

"If a parent were advised that a treatment with chloral hydrate or any drug like that was indicated, I would be much more concerned about the qualifications of the practitioner than the drug itself," says Paul Reggiardo, a spokesman for the American Academy of Pediatric Dentistry. "It's a drug with a very wide margin of safety."

Liquid sedatives are meant only to calm frightened or restless children enough so dentists can perform routine cavity-fillings or tooth extractions. Yet some dentists not only have been known to offer sedatives as a matter of course, in some instances they have upped the dose to dangerously

high levels.

"Often what happens is dentists find [a patient is] still ready to duke it out in the dental chair. It becomes easy to say 'Let's give him more,' "says Dave Anderson, chairman of the department of dental anesthesiology at Loma Linda University School of Dentistry.

High doses of sedatives can be devastating to the patient. Normally sedated patients can gag, breathe and swallow on their own. But if knocked unconscious from high doses, they may lose their ability to perform these protective reflexes and can die if they don't receive medical assistance.

Last September, a 3-year-old San Diego boy died after ingesting what investigators found to be a high dose of chloral hydrate.

In 1997, 4-year-old Javier Villa also died after being given a high dose of the sedative. The coroner investigating the case determined that the cause of death was asphyxiation.

When Hartmann and his colleagues reviewed oral-sedation mortality cases in California, they determined that most of the dentists involved had given higher doses of sedatives than they should have. Most failed to properly position their patients to keep their airways from becoming blocked. Few had even been monitoring the children's breathing. And none seemed to recognize the severity of the emergencies

When their patients' hearts stopped beating, the dentists tended to not know what to do, Hartmann says. Often CPR was not initiated. The dentists did not call 911 early enough. And some lied to paramedics about what they had given the children.

California has passed legislation requiring dentists to receive additional education before they can sedate patients younger than age 13. The law will take effect next January.

About the Author

Eros Pereira is Brazilian and now also Canadian. He lived in Brazil until he was 43, when he later emigrated to Canada with his family due to the incredible violence in the country. One can say this and refugee immigrants because they decide to leave the country to have more security for their family.

The author studied at Unicamp College for a year in Data Processing but had to leave school to start work at age 15. He finished College at the Anibal de Freitas State School in Campinas, São Paulo, where he completed the school while finishing his mandatory military service at the Army Cadet School.

Eros continued his military career by moving to the Army Sergeants School – ESIEx and then to ESSEx in Rio de Janeiro. After 5 years of service, the pious left the army and continued her dental school graduating in 1990 from the São Francisco University in Bragança Paulista.

He always enjoyed learning and studying; he continued his studies at The Paulista University, graduating in Law in 2000. After exercising law for three years together with dentistry. Due to his master's degree in Civil Law dedicated to teaching, he also graduated from the University of Campinas in Pedagogy.

Eros would still like to finish the physics course at the University of Campinas (Unicamp) because he always wanted science and connecting the universe. In addition, he is a science fiction enthusiast and has always read the classics of Isaac Asimov's fiction and so many other good authors.

The author currently lives in Canada and studies at Brigham Young Idaho University with the online programming engineering course. The author has three children and lives with his wife in Canada.

He participated in several courses in dentistry as improvement in orthodontics and endodontics. I studied English at Bow Valley College in Calgary, but I couldn't go back to any profession in Canada. The lives of immigrants have not been easy. Still, it has many rewards such as quality free health, high-level elementary education, and more than a developed country like Canada can offer.

The author is a Christian and attends church regularly. Survivors of the pandemic and now the difficulties generated by the wars, he hopes to be able to publish books that have not yet been released.

Contact: erospereira2@gmail.com

www.ingramcontent.com/pod-product-compliance
Lightning Source LLC
Chambersburg PA
CBHW060414220526
45465CB00008B/2883